THE
GREEN DIESEL YEARS

....

MARTIN JENKINS & CHARLES ROBERTS

Ian Allan
PUBLISHING

First published 2016

ISBN 978 0 7110 3831 8

Published by Ian Allan Publishing

an imprint of Ian Allan Publishing Ltd, 52/54 Hamm Moor Lane,
Addlestone, Surrey, KT15 2SF

Printed in Bulgaria

Visit the Ian Allan Publishing website at www.ianallanpubllshiing.com

FRONT COVER The first large diesel-electrics to appear
following publication of the British Transport Commission's
Modernisation Plan for BR were 10 English Electric Type 4s,
ordered as part of the Pilot Scheme and assigned to the Eastern
Region in 1958. The earliest examples were introduced on the
Great Eastern Section, but by the end of the year five were based
at Hornsey for working expresses on the East Coast main line.
In 1959 No D206 was photographed at Gamston Bank in charge
of an up train, the carriage liveries reflecting the changeover from
carmine-and-cream to crimson lake. *Derek Penney*

BACK COVER, UPPER The drive to replace steam led to the
construction of a range of diesel-electric locomotives with
different axle arrangements and within various power bands,
most being painted initially in green livery. Those found unreliable
or deemed surplus to requirements following the loss of traffic
were withdrawn first, but those that proved economical and easy
to maintain enjoyed long lives, and some remain in traffic today.
Among tho more successful were the English Electric Type 4s
introduced from 1958, one of which, No D386, is seen heading a
train of oil tankers near Shap towards the dying days of the green
livery, on 1 June 1971. *Les Folkard/Online Transport Archive*

BACK COVER, LOWER Construction of hundreds of new diesel
multiple-units began in 1954, presaging the Modernisation Plan.
Although built in BR workshops as well as by private contractors,
they were broadly similar. Power was mostly provided by two
150hp AEC or Leyland engines (often badged as BUT – British
United Traction) with six horizontal cylinders of varying sizes,
although some classes had more powerful Leyland Albion or
Rolls-Royce engines. This brand-new Derby-built high-density
set is seen at Merthyr Tydfil in 1957. Delivered in quantity to the
Western Region in 1957/8, these units transformed services in
the Cardiff Valleys. This early livery was unrelieved by bodyside
stripes or 'speed whiskers'. The white ends on the domed roofs
gave them a striking appearance when new but soon proved
difficult to clean. *Marcus Eavis/Online Transport Archive*

PREVIOUS PAGE This typical country scene from the 'green
diesel' era depicts a Cravens two-car DMU arriving at the
single-platform station of White Notley on a Braintree–Witham
working in 1964. Note the sparse nature of the building, the gas
lamps, the steps to assist people getting on and off … and the
sole intending passenger. Many hundreds of stations serving rural
communities were closed as a result of the Beeching Report,
but this line was reprieved and subsequently electrified, so that
in 2016 White Notley is served by an hourly through service to
London Liverpool Street. *Phil Tatt/Online Transport Archive*

INTRODUCTION

DEFINING THE 'GREEN DIESEL YEARS' IS NOT AN EXACT SCIENCE. When enthusiasts talk about 'the years of the Big Four' or 'the nationalised era' there are precise start and finish dates. The term 'green diesel years' derives from the range of liveries worn by British Railways diesel locomotives and multiple-units (DMUs) delivered from the mid-1950s in order to replace steam traction.

The new diesel era began with the 1955 Modernisation Plan – formally 'Modernisation and Re-Equipment of British Railways' – a radical project to invest heavily in new passenger and freight rolling stock and infrastructure whilst at the same time placing the railways on a secure financial footing. Within a few years the plans had foundered, and the parlous financial state of the nationalised rail network was deemed to need more drastic action. Enter, recruited from the private sector, Dr Richard Beeching, who, as BR Chairman, undertook a systematic review of the whole organisation. The outcome was the controversial 'Reshaping of British Railways' document of 1963 – known almost universally as the Beeching Report. Over the next 10 years or so this led to the elimination of approximately half of the network and the closure of thousands of stations, but it also heralded a new modern 'Inter-City' image built around the clean lines of blue locomotives and coaching stock. However, the green era took a long time to fade away and today is represented on a number of heritage railways.

In this book the authors have not set out to provide a definitive history of rolling stock types or liveries – there are many other books which provide that kind of authoritative reference material. Suffice to say that the period began with the railways already operating small numbers of diesel locomotives. The 'Big Four' had all introduced types of diesel shunter ahead of nationalisation in 1948, the LMS had placed in service one main-line diesel (No 10000), and other prototypes were on the drawing board. BR refined the concept of the diesel shunter and in 1952 rolled out the first of an eventual fleet of 1,193 350hp 0-6-0 diesel-electrics, some of which are still in operation today. Other shunters – a large proportion of them built to existing designs from private-sector manufacturers – were bought for specific applications, and many of these were destined to have short operational lives. Although used on the Continent for high-speed inter-city running as well as on lightly trafficked routes, diesel railcars found limited favour in Britain, only the GWR operating a small fleet, while the LMS built one three-car unit.

Although steam-locomotive production would continue until 1960 the Modernisation Plan initiated the wide-scale transition to diesel and, in a Pilot Scheme, some 174 locomotives of various specifications were ordered, initially in three power bands, although these would later be extended, eventually ranging from Type 1 (up to 1,000hp) for local freight work to Type 5 (3,000hp and above) for express passenger. The first of the Modernisation Plan diesels (English Electric Type 1 No D8000) did not enter service until 1957, by which time the decision had already been made to place significant orders for each type, from both BR workshops and the private sector, many of which were rushed into service with insufficient testing. Regions were allowed a certain degree of autonomy, which led, for example, to the 'Deltics' and various Western Region (WR) diesel-hydraulics being concentrated in particular parts of the country. By the mid-1960s there were more than 20 classes of main-line locomotive in service, some of which had already required major re-engineering, and several were rendered obsolete by the decline in traffic resulting from the impact of the Beeching Report. The last new class delivered in green – the Swindon-built Type 1 0-6-0 – was destined to have the shortest life of all.

Post-nationalisation railcar development led to the privately financed ACV Demonstration Train, which ran on the London Midland Region (LMR) between 1952 and 1959. This was followed by a batch of 'Lightweight' DMUs from Derby Works in 1954 for use in West Yorkshire, followed by a range of designs from both BR workshops and private manufacturers. As with the locomotives, teething problems or non-standard features led to the early withdrawal of several types. The rather haphazard approach to rolling-stock planning and procurement is highlighted by the short history of the four-wheeled railbuses. It was hoped that these low-cost vehicles would allow for the economic retention of certain branch lines, but after the delivery of 22 vehicles from no fewer than five different manufacturers in 1958/9, all were withdrawn by 1968.

In this volume the authors have aimed to capture the spirit of the 'green diesel' years with a series of evocative colour scenes – the vast majority of which have not previously been published – covering a journey from the West of Scotland to Cornwall. They have tried to include as many types of locomotive, DMU, railcar and railbus from the period, although they have not attempted to cover every variant. The selected images feature trains in a variety of settings – rural and urban, in service and on shed, hauling freight and carrying passengers, some on bright sunny days and some in rain and cloud. There are scenes of locomotives in build, in service, in store and on the cusp of being despatched to the breaker's yard. The authors have included transitional scenes featuring steam alongside diesel and, as a reminder of some of the less-attractive aspects of the era, have included a few views of locomotives in appalling external condition.

Its title notwithstanding, not everything in the book is in green. Some of the Great Western Railway (GWR) railcars, for example, were carmine-and-cream, whilst diesel shunters introduced prior to nationalisation were painted in unlined black, and this continued well into the BR era. In 1954 a green livery was applied to the first of the new DMUs, and within a few years this had become standard colour for most diesel locomotives as well. However, there were many variants, and even today it is difficult to reach agreement on shades and names. The colour applied to early Modernisation Plan locomotives is often described as Brunswick green, as used on steam locomotives, although there is debate about the official status of this name. During the years covered by the book some locomotives and DMUs appeared in other colours, some of which appear in these pages, to say nothing of the yellow warning panels and 'speed whiskers' of different shapes and sizes as they were introduced to aid visibility and safety. Furthermore, the authors make only occasional reference to colour shades. The combined factors of different paint manufacturers and applications, fading, discolouring and general grime – not to mention mistaken memories, different rendition on film and the effect of sunlight and other illumination – makes it impossible to be definitive on colour.

In order to give a contemporaneous feel to the captions the authors have generally used the designations which were in use at the time rather than the later TOPS classes, although occasional reference has been made to the latter in the case of locomotives which survive today. Likewise, train times have been given in 12-hour-clock form rather than the 24-hour system that was adopted by BR in 1964/5.

The authors wish to thank the large number of people who have helped with the production of this book but especially Jean Atkinson, Jonathan Cadwallader, Neil Davenport, David Jenkins, Gavin Morrison, Jon Penn (for facilitating access to Edgar Richards' collection), Derek Penney, Hamish Stevenson, David Ventry and Peter Waller.

An extensive bibliography has been used in connection with the writing and verifying of the text, including *A Pictorial Record of the Diesel Shunter* by Colin J. Marsden (OPC, 1981), *British Rail DMUs and Diesel Railcars* by Brian Morrison (Ian Allan, 1998), *British Rail Main Line Diesel Locomotives* by Colin J. Marsden and Graham B. Fenn (OPC, 1988), *British Railways First Generation DMUs* by Hugh Longworth (OPC, 2011), *BR Diesel and Locomotives for Scrap* by Ashley Butlin (OPC, 2015), *Locomotive Directory* by Colin J. Marsden (OPC, 1991), *BR Diesel Traction in Scotland* by George C. O'Hara (Clyard Novella, 2011), *BR First Generation Diesel Railbuses* by Evan Green-Hughes (Ian Allan, 2011), *Diesel Pioneers* by David N. Clough (Ian Allan, 2005), *English Electric Main Line Diesel Locomotives of British Rail* by Brian Webb (David & Charles, 1976), and *Locomotive Directory* by D. C. Strickland (Diesel & Electric Group, 1983). Ian Allan 'ABC' combined volumes covering the entire period provided valuable

ABOVE

During the transition from steam to diesel traction BR allowed its Regions a degree of autonomy, with the result that the Western opted for diesel-hydraulic instead of diesel-electric designs. One of the Swindon-built diesel-hydraulic Type 4 'Warships' is pictured at Waterloo during the period (1964-71) when these locomotives provided the motive power for the service to Exeter St Davids. No D826 *Jupiter* was in traffic from September 1960 to October 1971, clocking up more than one million miles in service. *Phil Tatt/Online Transport Archive*

data, whilst websites such as www.railuk.info and www.class47.co.uk have helped enormously with individual locomotive histories. Network information has been provided by reference to *British Railways Pre-Grouping Atlas and Gazetteer* by W. Philip Conolly (Ian Allan, 1958), *Rail Atlas of Britain and Ireland* by Stuart Baker (OPC, various editions), *Rail Atlas: The Beeching Era* by Peter Waller (Ian Allan, 2013), *Dr Beeching's Axe 50 Years On* by Julian Holland (David & Charles, 2013), *Passengers No More* by Gerald Daniels and Les Dench (Ian Allan, 1980 – third edition), and *The Railways of Great Britain: A Historical Atlas* by Col M. H. Cobb (Ian Allan, 2003).

The Green Diesel Years has been produced as a fund-raising project for Online Transport Archive, a registered charity founded in 2000 to ensure the preservation of collections of photographs and moving images. Both authors are directors and trustees of OTA and have donated their fees to the Archive. If you are looking for a home for your own collection or would like details relating to OTA please see our website – www.onlinetransportatchive.com – or write to The Secretary, 25 Monkmoor Road, Shrewsbury SY2 5AG.

The book is dedicated to Edgar Richards, who for some 70 years has recorded so many aspects of the railway scene.

MARTIN JENKINS   CHARLES ROBERTS
Walton-on-Thames   Upton, Wirral

This journey through the 'green diesel' years begins at Kyle of Lochalsh, terminus of one of the country's most spectacular railways. Our first view features Derby-built No D5127 waiting to depart with the 5.30pm to Inverness on 3 August 1966. This was one of a large number of BR Type 2 Bo-Bo locomotives built by Crewe, Darlington and Derby Works between 1958 and 1967 and by Beyer, Peacock & Co between 1965 and 1967. The early examples (Nos D5000-5150) had 1,160hp Sulzer engines, the later machines (Nos D5151-5299 and D7500-7677) uprated 1,250hp units. This locomotive was in traffic from 1960 until 1976.
Martin Jenkins/Online Transport Archive

The second view at Kyle, recorded on 31 August 1964, shows a tablet-catcher in the recess on the driver's cab side of Type 2 Bo-Bo No D5344. These devices, installed at St Rollox Works in Glasgow, were carried by several classes working on the many single-track sections on the Scottish Region. Built by the Birmingham Railway Carriage & Wagon Works (BRCW) at Smethwick, this locomotive was one of 47 (Nos D5300-46) introduced during 1958/9 with 1,160hp Sulzer engines, nose-end communicating doors (which were never used) and train-identifying headcode discs.
John Worley/Online Transport Archive

Allocated to Scotland in 1961, Nos D5347-69 were the earliest examples of a class of 69 BRCW Type 2 Bo-Bo locomotives (Nos D5347-5415) with 1,250hp Sulzer engines. Overlooked by the Pap of Glencoe, No D5349 waits to leave Ballachulish on 2 August 1965 with the 4.20pm to Oban; note the fitted snowploughs, which could clear small drifts during the winter months. Listed in the Beeching Report, this well-engineered branch closed to goods in June 1965 and to passengers in late March 1966; for many years it had transported stone from the quarry seen in the background, which also had its own internal rail system. The locomotive would remain in traffic until 1987. *E. V. Richards*

As part of the pilot scheme for new diesels, the North British Locomotive Co (NBL) secured an order for 10 Type 2 Bo-Bo locomotives for main-line passenger and freight operations. This order was later increased, a total of 58 (Nos D6100-57) entering service in the period 1958-60, all eventually being assigned to Scotland. Unfortunately their MAN four-stroke engines caused major problems, so from 1963 20 were re-equipped with more powerful Paxman units. However, No D6149, seen at Maud on 2 August 1963 whilst working the service to Peterhead, was one of those to retain its original 1,100hp engine until withdrawn, in December 1967.

The Cravens DMU was working the 12.30pm from Fraserburgh to Aberdeen. Despite the introduction of diesel traction in 1959 the lines from Dyce to Peterhead and Fraserburgh were listed in the Beeching Report and closed to passengers during 1965, although freight would continue to Peterhead until 1970 and to Fraserburgh until 1979. *John Ryan*

To replace steam on cross-country services 194 DMU vehicles (130 motor cars and 64 trailers) were built by the BR works at Swindon in the period 1957-60, and seven three-car sets were allocated to Kittybrewster depot for services in northeast Scotland. In April 1968 one such formation, SC51781 leading, stops at Elgin while on an Inverness–Aberdeen service. A yellow band above the windows indicated First class. Later, as the rail network contracted, these units were reassigned to services for which they had not been built. *Alan Trotter/Eastbank Model Railway Club*

Among the private-sector firms contracted to build DMUs was Sheffield-based Cravens, which in the years 1956-60 produced 402 vehicles. Here, on 8 September 1960, a two-car unit headed by Driving Trailer Composite SC56463, passes through Inverurie, once the headquarters of the Great North of Scotland Railway. In the yard can be seen a variety of four-wheel vans.
Ian Dunnett/Online Transport Archive

One of the unsuccessful class of 58 NBL Type 2 Bo-Bo locomotives, No D6152 was photographed at Inverurie when just three months old, on 8 September 1960. This was another example to retain its original engine until withdrawn in August 1968. The entire class was eventually based in Scotland so that they could be easily returned to the NBL works in the event of a major failure.
Ian Dunnett/Online Transport Archive

An interesting 'one-off' was this experimental battery-electric unit consisting of a Motor Brake Second (SC79998) and Driving Trailer Composite (SC79999). Before entering service the two Derby-built vehicles were sent to Cowlairs Works to be fitted with batteries and Siemens electrical equipment. In April 1958 the set was photographed waiting to depart Aberdeen for Ballater. After the branch closed to passengers in 1966 this unit was taken into departmental service and was subsequently preserved.
Phil Tatt/Online Transport Archive

The attractive 43½-mile line along the Dee Valley had reached Ballater in 1866. Plans to extend to Braemar were opposed by Queen Victoria and were never implemented, although the Royal Family and their guests made frequent use of the line until 1965. In common with many other rural branch lines it suffered from a postwar slump in traffic and was listed for closure in the Beeching Report, passenger traffic to Ballater ceasing in February 1966, to be followed by freight in July 1967. Following closure the impressive station was retained as a museum, but in 2015 it was almost entirely destroyed by fire. *John Ryan*

LEFT

On 2 August 1966 a Cravens twin, SC56479 leading, passes a sister unit at Dufftown, in the heart of a whisky-producing area. Located between Keith Junction and Craigellachie, this station would close to passengers in May 1968. On the platform, staff wait to load goods, whilst in the background are the sidings which continued to serve Associated British Maltsters until 1985, after which the tracks were used by privately sponsored excursion trains until 1991. Today they form part of the Keith & Dufftown Railway, which trades as 'The Whisky Line'.
Martin Jenkins/Online Transport Archive

ABOVE

In an attempt to prevent the closure of some uneconomic lines BR experimented with four-wheel diesel railbuses. Cars 79970-4 were built by Park Royal Vehicles and originally assigned to the London Midland Region before being transferred to Scotland. Still displaying its LMR 'M' prefix, 79973 pauses at deserted Advie station on 18 August 1965 whilst working along the attractive Spey Valley, which for many years handled traffic from various distilleries as well as coal and timber. When the railbuses were introduced in 1959 several new halts were opened, and passenger loadings increased by 88%, but the service was too sparse, and the line closed to passengers in October 1965 and to goods in November 1971. The last of these railbuses was withdrawn in early 1967, 79973 eking out its final months shuttling between Buxton and Miller's Dale.
Martin Jenkins/Online Transport Archive

A pair of BR Type 2s emit a throaty roar as they accelerate away from Pitlochry in the summer of 1960. For some duties these locomotives were found to be underpowered, so they frequently worked in pairs on more steeply graded lines.
J. N. Barlow/Online Transport Archive

Derby-built Type 2 No D5114 stands at Aberfeldy, terminus of the attractive 8¾-mile branch from Ballinluig, on 3 April 1964 with a single ex-LMS carriage, two wagons and a brake van. This seemingly bucolic scene highlights many of the economic problems facing the railway. The train would have had a driver, second man and guard, while the station is well-kept and clearly still manned, the only problem being an absence of passengers and goods traffic sufficient to sustain the service. This branch, with its six return workings and 40 bridges, closed to goods in January 1965 and to passengers in May of the same year. No D5114 was the first BR Type 2 to be delivered to Scotland, in April 1960, and was also the first of the class to have the four-character headcode box in lieu of identification discs. It was destined to remain in traffic until 1973.
I. G. Holt

Among the railbuses working in Scotland were SC79965-9, built in 1958 by D. Wickham & Co of Ware, Hertfordshire, and powered by 105hp six-cylinder Meadows engines. They featured pneumatic suspension, retractable steps for ease of access, a central headlight and 'dumb buffers' made of sprung metal bands. Here SC79968 rests at Crieff, waiting to depart for Gleneagles, in June 1960. Because of reliability problems with the various types of railbus, steam was often substituted on this line until its closure to passengers in July 1964, goods traffic ceasing in November. By early 1965 the 48-seater Wickhams were surplus to requirements, and all had been scrapped by the end of the following year.
A. S. Clayton/Online Transport Archive

Named or titled trains have always lent a certain glamour to the railways. In 1964, English Electric (EE) Type 4 1Co-Co1 No D362 pauses at Stirling with the southbound 'Saint Mungo' from Aberdeen to Glasgow Buchanan Street. Under the Modernisation Plan's Pilot Scheme 10 of these 2,000hp express locomotives were ordered from EE and assembled by the Vulcan Foundry at Newton-le-Willows, the first entering service in March 1958. They were soon followed by a further 190 examples, all but 20 built at Vulcan Foundry. The entire class (Nos D200-399) had EE engines and electrical equipment. Delivered in October 1961, No D362 was one of the later examples with centrally positioned alphanumeric headcode displays. It would be withdrawn at the end of 1982. *Harry Luff/Online Transport Archive*

To cater for 'Inter-City' work in Scotland, in 1956 the BR Works at Swindon produced a mixed fleet of motor and trailer cars, which could be operated as three- or six-car trains. Here a six-car formation leaves Glasgow Queen Street for Edinburgh in 1960. Note the cab-window arrangement, the bracket for the single-character headcode stencil, the absence of destination blinds and marker lights and the obligatory oil tail lamp. As traffic increased these units were replaced by locomotive-hauled trains.

W. J. Wyse/LRTA (London Area)

One of the most reliable classes of diesel-electric locomotive was the EE Type 1 Bo-Bo, some of which are still active in 2016. Altogether 228 (Nos D8000-8199 and No D8300-27) were built in the years 1957-62 and 1966-8, most at Vulcan Foundry but also by Robert Stephenson & Hawthorn. Working cab-first, No D8122 approaches its home depot of Polmadie in June 1968. In service from 1962 until 1991, this locomotive was eventually scrapped not far from where the photograph was taken, by MC Metals at Springburn.

Alan Trotter/Eastbank Model Railway Club

Resting between duties at Hamilton on 20 July 1961 is one of a pair of railbuses built by Bristol Commercial Vehicles and bodied by Eastern Coach Works. These featured bus-style seats and windows, while hiding the underframe was a valance incorporating a headlamp beneath the chromium-plated fender. Power was provided by a 112hp Gardner 6HLW engine. Entering service in 1958, SC79958 and SC79959 spent their working lives in Scotland. Rough riders, they proved unreliable and were out of service by the end of 1964, albeit not officially withdrawn. Both were scrapped two years later.
Jim Oatway

Although DMUs helped reduce running costs they failed to save many lines from closure. Until October 1964 passengers could travel southwest from Lanark to Muirkirk, but the sparse nature of the weekday service saw the line listed for closure in the Beeching Report. However, the Glasgow service was retained, and on 28 August 1965 a Cravens twin unit formed of SC51484 and SC56473 was captured awaiting departure from Lanark as the 10.55am to Glasgow Central. Today the town is served by a half-hourly electric service to Glasgow Central High Level.
E. V. Richards

Among the first DMUs to operate in Scotland were from a batch of 40 semi-lightweight two-car units, designed for local and branch-line work and built in 1957/8 by the Gloucester Railway Carriage & Wagon Co, the motor cars having two 150hp six-cylinder engines. On 28 August 1965, a Gloucester twin, Driving Motor Brake Second SC50345 leading, waits at gas-lit East Kilbride with the 8.50pm to Glasgow St Enoch as a porter busily unloads parcels and other goods. The last of these units would remain in traffic until 1989.
E. V. Richards

This fine study of EE Type 5 Co-Co No D9004 in two-tone green dates from 14 October 1961, just a few months after the locomotive was delivered from Vulcan Foundry. It was one of a stud of eight 'Deltics' assigned to Haymarket shed to work crack East Coast expresses between Edinburgh Waverley and King's Cross. Capable of speeds in excess of 100mph, they had two Napier Deltic power units giving a combined output of 3,300hp, electrical equipment being supplied by EE. Midway along the body can be seen the BR emblem, which would be displaced by the nameplate *Queen's Own Highlander* in May 1964, when No D9004 was named after the Scottish regiment. Withdrawal came in November 1981, after just over 20 years of service. *Ian Dunnett/Online Transport Archive*

The 117 centre-cab 'Claytons' were among the least successful locomotives ordered by BR. Nos D8500-87 were built between 1962 and 1965 by the Clayton Equipment Co, and Nos D8588-8616 by Beyer, Peacock & Co of Manchester during 1964/5. Many were allocated to Scotland, among them No D8578, seen shunting at Haddington on 1 June 1964, just three months after entering traffic. This view shows the two-tone livery, with lighter green applied to the upper areas. Like so many of the class No D8578 remained in BR service for only a very short time, being withdrawn in June 1969. The short Haddington branch lost its passenger service in 1949 and freight in 1968. *John Ryan*

Amongst many different types of shunter to operate in Scotland were some from a class of eight diesel-hydraulic 0-4-0s (Nos 11700-7, later D2700-7) built by NBL and delivered in two batches, in 1953/4 and 1955/6. Assigned to Edinburgh St Margarets shed, No 11706 is seen working within Leith Docks in 1959; note the builder's distinctive diamond plate, discernible just below the number. The locomotive was withdrawn as No D2706 in March 1967. *Ian Dunnett/Online Transport Archive*

Early 'dieselisation' in the Edinburgh area is represented by a 1959 Derby-built two-car unit passing Craigentinny sidings *en route* to Edinburgh Waverley on 2 July 1960. Waiting to leave the sidings with an empty stock working is North British 'J37' 0-6-0 No 64608. Steam would bow out in Scotland at the end of 1966. *Ian Dunnett/Online Transport Archive*

A pair of BRCW Type 2 Bo-Bo locomotives, No D5317 leading, pull out of Craigentinny sidings with an empty-stock working for Edinburgh Waverley in July 1961. Although blending in well with the overall design the communicating doors (which enabled the second man to pass between the locomotives to deal with any problems when working in multiple, as seen here) were later removed. Following modifications the class proved successful and would be familiar throughout Scotland for 30 years, although No D5317, new in February 1959, was destined to remain in service only until August 1977. *Ian Dunnett/Online Transport Archive*

Between 1956 and 1960 the Metropolitan-Cammell Carriage & Wagon Co provided BR with the largest number of DMUs produced by the private sector – 637 vehicles, of which 364 were powered. This allowed for the operation of two-, three- or four-car units, and in due course they would be seen over most of the network. In the first view Driving Trailer Composite E56073 (leading) and Driving Motor Composite E50268 wait to leave Haltwhistle as the noon departure to Alston on 19 April 1965. Despite being listed for closure before publication of the Beeching Report this branch survived until 1976 owing to the unsuitability of the local roads to take the replacing buses. In the second photograph, taken from Gateshead, a four-car formation has just left Newcastle Central and is crossing over the Tyne on the High Level Bridge, heading for South Shields. Across the river can be seen The Keep, the Cathedral Church of St Nicholas and, in the distance (left), the floodlights of St James' Park, home of Newcastle United FC. *E. V. Richards; Marcus Eavis/Online Transport Archive*

LEFT

Synonymous with the North Eastern Region from 1961, the English Electric Type 3 Co-Co, powered by EE's own 1,750hp 12-cylinder engine, was among the most numerous of the early diesel designs, no fewer than 309 examples (Nos D6700-6999 and D6600-8) being built, mostly at Vulcan Foundry but also by Robert Stephenson & Hawthorns. For decades the North East of England was a hive of labour-intensive industries served by a complex rail network, and in the first view, recorded in 1967, No D6761 is seen in at Cargo Fleet, then a centre for iron and steel, petrochemicals and oil refining. This locomotive was in traffic from 1962 to 2001, after which it was leased to work on a Spanish infrastructure project, finally being cut up at Vilafranca del Penedes in 2011. The second photograph, taken at Hart, features another Type 3 hauling a rake of loaded mineral wagons, having come from the direction of Castle Eden on a line that would close in 1979. The headcode denotes a Class 7 partially fitted freight permitted to travel at 45mph, the tender being needed to provide additional braking effort. In the third picture an example built by RSH has stopped at Eaglescliffe whilst working a charter on 19 June 1965. First allocated to Thornaby shed, in July 1962, it has early split headcode boxes located either side of the nose-end gangway doors. Latterly known as Class 37, these locomotives were arguably the most successful diesels of their era, many being still extant in 2016; following a spell in France No D6769 (as 37069) remains in traffic in the fleet of Direct Rail Services. *G. D. Smith/ Online Transport Archive; Phil Tatt/Online Transport Archive; E. V. Richards*

ABOVE

The 22 'Deltics' were shared between the Scottish, North Eastern and Eastern Regions, those allocated to the latter eventually being named after famous racehorses. Here one such locomotive, No D9003 *Meld*, approaches Darlington Bank Top with the up 'Heart of Midlothian' on 17 April 1965. Although reliable the 'Deltics' were expensive to maintain, and following the introduction of High Speed Trains on the East Coast main line in the late 1970s they were displaced from top-link workings. No D9003 spent its working life at Finsbury Park and was in service from March 1961 to December 1980, ultimately being scrapped in March 1981. Six production-series 'Deltics' survive in preservation. *E. V. Richards*

RIGHT

Shunting within soot-encrusted York station is No D2046, one of a class of 230 diesel-mechanical locomotives built by BR at Doncaster and Swindon Works in the years 1957-62. Powered by 204hp Gardner engines, these reliable 0-6-0s could be found in large numbers on the Eastern and North Eastern Regions. This Doncaster-built example was in traffic from 1958 to 1971.
J. L. May/Online Transport Archive

Crossing to Carlisle, old and new occupy the centre roads on
2 July 1965, the station pilot, Ivatt 2-6-2 tank No 41217, being
seen alongside an early Derby 'Lightweight'. The latter was one of
102 such units introduced from 1954, the motor cars each having
two 150hp engines and a pre-selector gearbox. Assigned at first
to duties in West Cumberland, they included two- and four-car
sets. The Yellow Diamond coupling code was an early standard
but was soon superseded by others, most commonly Blue
Square. As a result these units were restricted in their ability to
work in multiple with other types of DMU, which fact led to their
withdrawal as non-standard by the end of the 1960s.
Neil Caplan/Online Transport Archive

On 8 September 1959 a Metro-Cammell DMU, E50257
leading, has stopped at Appleby East whilst working one
of the handful of all-stations, cross-country services linking
Penrith with Darlington, a journey of some 65 miles. The suffix
'East' was added in the early 1950s to distinguish it from the
nearby station on the Settle–Carlisle line. Passenger trains last
served Appleby East in January 1962, regular freight continuing
until June 1967, after which the line through the station was
used only occasionally, for quarry, military and excursion
traffic. Eventually it was mothballed, the station site remaining
largely intact. *Mrs E. D. Davenport*

Ordered as part of the 1955 Modernisation Plan, the 20 Type 2s built by Metropolitan Vickers at Stockton-on-Tees were unusual and short-lived. Entering service during 1958/9, they had one six-wheel and one four-wheel bogie (Co-Bo) and were powered by 1,200hp two-stroke Crossley engines. Reliability problems and trouble with the engines resulted in the entire class (Nos D5700-19) being stored during most of 1961 prior to improvements being undertaken, after which they found employment in the North West of England. The last of the class, No D5719, heads a train of mineral wagons through Millom in March 1968, just months before withdrawal. All 20 of these non-standard Type 2s were withdrawn in 1967/8, just one being repainted in BR's new standard blue livery. *Alan Atkinson/Online Transport Archive*

ABOVE

On Saturday 29 August 1964 No D5705 passes through Morecambe South Junction with the 10.53am Workington Main–Euston service. Upon arrival at Preston at 2.45pm the locomotive would be replaced for the onward journey south. Following withdrawal No D5705 was used by BR's Research Division at Derby and was later used to pre-heat carriages. Purchased subsequently for preservation, it is still under restoration, currently (2016) at the East Lancashire Railway. *Gavin Morrison*

The demanding Settle–Carlisle line provides photographers with a wide range of locations. With Wild Boar Fell in the background, 'Peak' No D115 growls past Ais Gill Summit with the up 'Thames-Clyde Express' on 4 April 1965. This was one of the later' Peaks', lacking nose-end doors and with a central headcode box, and was in traffic from August 1961 to July 1977. *Gavin Morrison*

Amongst the many outstanding structures on the challenging Settle–Carlisle line is Smardale Viaduct, to the north of Kirkby Stephen. In this view an unidentified BR Type 4 'Peak' heads north with the down 'Thames–Clyde Express'. In the early 1960s this took nearly nine hours to complete the journey from London St Pancras to Glasgow St Enoch and gained a reputation for poor time-keeping and slow running; the title was last used in 1974. Following the delivery in 1959/60 of 10 'Peak' 1Co-Co1 locomotives (Nos D1-10) with 2,300hp Sulzer engines an order was placed for a further 127 (D11-137) with uprated (2,500hp) power units, and these were built variously at Crewe and Derby in the years 1960-3. *Derek Penney*

ABOVE

In another view recorded on 4 April 1965 No D336 approaches Blea Moor with the diverted down 'Royal Scot'. This was one of 20 EE Type 4s built in 1960/1 with headcode boxes on either side of the nose-end communicating doors. Delivered from Vulcan Foundry in March 1961, it would be withdrawn in May 1982.
Gavin Morrison

BELOW

Penyghent forms the backdrop in this powerful portrait of No 5097 (its 'D' prefix having been dropped with the end of steam) as it grinds slowly uphill past Horton-in-Ribblesdale on the long climb to Ribblehead Viaduct and Blea Moor on 29 November 1969. This Darlington-built BR standard Type 2 was in traffic from May 1960 to February 1976. *Gavin Morrison*

From 1959 EE Type 4s were assigned to the LMR to start the process of replacing steam on a wide range of express workings, including prestigious named trains such as the 'Royal Scot', which ran daily between Euston and Glasgow Central. Sometimes, however, the new form of traction struggled on some of the more demanding sections of line, and on

7 August 1961 No D313 was making heavy weather of the climb up to Shap Summit, on the West Coast main line. Note the nameboard and the headcode discs set to show it was operating a Class 1 express. This locomotive was in traffic from December 1960 until October 1981. The 'Royal Scot' last ran in 2003.
Gavin Morrison

For a relatively small town Southport had a large number of stations, one of which, St Luke's, had no fewer than four names during its existence. It consisted of two island platforms located some distance apart. Outbound from Southport, a BRCW three-car DMU is seen on the direct Wigan tracks shortly before these were closed in June 1965, services being re-routed over the former line to Preston (left), where the third rail used by the local electric service to Crossens until September 1964 was still *in situ*. St Luke's finally closed in September 1968, although the tracks on the left are still in regular use. *J. G. Parkinson/Online Transport Archive*

On 5 August 1967 a Brush Type 4 hauls a Freightliner through Tebay. Some 512 of these powerful Co-Co locomotives were built in the years 1962-7 – the majority (310) at the Falcon Works in Loughborough, the remainder by BR at Crewe – and as such they formed the largest single main-line class. The 2,750hp Sulzer engines, built under licence by Vickers at Barrow, were later derated to 2,580hp to improve reliability and reduce maintenance costs. *Peter Jackson*

Following the postwar strengthening of the swing bridge giving access to Princes Dock, Liverpool, heavier locomotives could reach to Riverside station, which had been opened by the Mersey Docks & Harbour Board in 1895 to provide a rail/ship interchange for London & North Western Railway boat trains. Having descended from Edge Hill station to Waterloo Goods, EE Type 4 No D379 has just crossed the busy Dock Road and is now proceeding at snail's space across the bridge in 1964. Riverside closed in 1971, and most of the dockland buildings in the background have since been demolished, although some of the Victorian warehouses on the left are now apartments. No D379 was in traffic from 1962 to 1981.

B. D. Pyne/Online Transport Archive

Built at Vulcan Foundry, DP2 (Diesel Prototype 2) first emerged in early 1962. Although fitted with a modified 'Deltic' body, this impressive Co-Co machine had radically different internal equipment, including an EE power unit capable of producing 2,700hp. During a comprehensive range of tests it proved sufficiently reliable to operate at times without an EE engineer. In the summer of 1962 it waits to leave Liverpool Lime Street with the 'Manxman', the 2.5pm non-stop express to Euston. Following a major overhaul in 1965 it was repainted in 'Deltic'-style two-tone green and then in 1966 fitted with new advanced forms of control equipment, but following a serious accident in July 1967 it returned to EE, which scrapped it the following year. Overall, DP2 was a success and was essentially the forerunner of the later Type 4s (Class 50s). *J. N. Barlow/Online Transport Archive*

Three views illustrating the variety of shunters employed in and around Merseyside. In the first No D2553 makes for Garston docks with a rake of mineral wagons on 5 May 1967. This was from a class of 69 diesel-mechanical 0-6-0s powered by Gardner 8L3 engines and built by the Hunslet Engine Co during the period 1955-61. In the second photograph 12014 is at work at Garston on 23 October 1963. This was one of 40 diesel-electric 0-6-0s (Nos 7080-7119) powered by EE 350hp engines and built by the London, Midland & Scottish Railway at Derby Works between 1939 and 1942. After 10 were transferred to the War Department those taken into BR stock were eventually renumbered 12003-32. With a top speed of 20mph they were ideal for moving heavy trains, especially coal, between the reception sidings and the dockside. Note the jackshaft connection in front of the rear wheels, the array of lamps on the running plate and a shunter's pole for coupling and uncoupling wagons. The last of these former LMS shunters was withdrawn in 1967. The third picture shows No D2219, one of 141 diesel-mechanical 0-6-0s supplied in the years 1952-61 by the Drewry Car Co. Here it waits to lead a mixed convoy across Duke Street in the heart of Birkenhead's dockland in September 1967. In the heyday of the docks this road/rail intersection was so busy that it had to be controlled 24 hours a day, seven days a week, by a policeman on point duty, who liaised directly with railway employees who, armed with red flags, stopped the traffic. *E. V. Richards; G. D. Smith/Online Transport Archive; Martin Jenkins/Online Transport Archive*

Three different types of DMU occupy the platforms at Birkenhead Woodside shortly before this five-platform terminus, with its impressive iron-arched trainshed, closed in November 1967. On the left is a relatively rare Park Royal two-car set, one of 20 delivered in 1957/8, the other units being a Metro-Cammell (centre) and a Gloucester (right). These would have been working local services to Chester, Hooton and Helsby.
Marcus Eavis/Online Transport Archive

With the elimination of steam the 'D' prefix to diesel-locomotive numbers became redundant. With its 'D' crudely obliterated, No 7635 rests between duties at Mollington Street shed, Birkenhead, in company with No D7633. These were among 327 BR Type 2s, with 1,250hp Sulzer engines, which entered service in the period 1961-7. Although the majority were built at either Derby or Darlington 36 of these locomotives, including the pair seen here, were constructed by Beyer Peacock in 1965/6. Later examples such as these had grilles above the cantrail (as opposed to in the body side) and lacked nose-end doors, which modifications gave them a neater overall appearance. Both would be withdrawn in the late 1980s. *E. V. Richards*

A charming study of a Derby-built DMU on a Wrexham Central–Chester Northgate service calling at Caergwrle Castle & Wells station during Easter 1967. Note the Blue Square coupling code, the letters 'LW' indicating that this is a lightweight unit. Although listed for closure in the Beeching Report the Wrexham–Bidston line, including Caergwrle, survived, but the section from Dee Marsh Junction to Chester Northgate lost its passenger service in September 1968. The signalbox was last used in 1982, and the station buildings have long since gone, being replaced by more rudimentary facilities. *Phil Tatt/Online Transport Archive*

Speeding along the North Wales coast near Abergele on 30 August 1966 on a service from Crewe to Bangor and Carnarvon is a six-car DMU made up of two Derby twin sets topping-and-tailing a Metro-Cammell unit. To handle the heavy holiday traffic to and from the area's many resorts there were, for many years, four tracks along most of this busy line. *E. V. Richards*

In 1956 BR took delivery of five short-wheelbase 0-4-0 shunters built by Andrew Barclay and powered by Gardner 153hp engines. Four were taken into capital stock and eventually numbered D2953-6, two being allocated to Holyhead for operating an entirely isolated line which had its own shed and facilities and was used to transport heavy stones to reinforce a breakwater. The pair survived long enough to be included in the 1973 renumbering scheme as Class 01, the former D2955 (originally 11505) being seen here on 18 December 1974. This pair always retained the standard black livery worn by shunters before the green era, complete with the original lion-over-wheel BR emblem, the yellow and black warning stripes being the only concession to the new style. The line closed in 1980 when lorries took over the work, and No 01 002, latterly the only operable locomotive, was duly scrapped on site in 1982. *E. V. Richards*

Heading a parcels train from Holyhead, Crewe-built Brush Type 4 No D1848 makes its way out of Llandudno Junction station on 17 July 1965. This important link providing rail access to the steamers sailing to Ireland had opened in 1848, the junction station opening 10 years later along with the branch into the resort itself. The Brush Type 4s were painted in a stylish, specially designed livery of two-tone green. Virtually brand-new when photographed, this example had entered traffic in June 1965 and would survive until badly damaged by fire in 1989.

G. D. Smith/Online Transport Archive

Flanked by GWR signals and signalbox in August 1967, No D5140 rumbles towards Morfa Mawddach station (formerly Barmouth Junction) at the head of a loose-coupled goods train which has just crossed Afon Mawddach by way of Barmouth Bridge. This whole site has now been scaled down and the former four-platform junction station reduced to an unstaffed halt. Built at Derby with roof-mounted headcode boxes, No D5140 was among the last of the 151 1,160hp BR Type 2s to enter service, in November 1960, and would remain in traffic until January 1976.

R. W. A. Jones/Online Transport Archive

ABOVE

EE Type 4 No D373 waits for signal clearance as it heads a permanent-way train through Weston Rhyn, on the line between Wrexham and Chirk, in March 1967, the sidings on the right serving nearby collieries. It is on one of the loops which existed on either side of the main line; along with the signals and signalbox these loops were subsequently removed. This Type 4 was from the final batch of 55 locomotives built at Vulcan Foundry and was in traffic from 1962 until 1981.

Phil Tatt/Online Transport Archive

BELOW

Waiting to leave Church Stretton in the early 1960s on a southbound service to Cardiff is a Swindon-built 'Cross-Country' three-car DMU, the stock being among the 130 motor cars and 64 trailers of this type built between 1957 and 1960. In later years DMUs working the Central Wales line were fitted with a powerful headlight between the cab windows. The last of these units was withdrawn in 1989. All these traditional station buildings have since been demolished.

G. W. Morant/Online Transport Archive

Some Beeching closures sparked strong local opposition. One such case involved the frequent, well-patronised service to Bacup, which had been worked by DMUs since 1956, most trains running to either Bury or Manchester Victoria. On the last day of service, in early December 1966, Bacup station exuded an air of desolation. Goods traffic had ended in November 1964, and local coal deliveries ceased in May 1966. The first view shows one of 25 two-car Cravens sets built in 1959 for use on steeply graded lines, each car having a powerful (238hp) eight-cylinder Rolls-Royce engine with hydraulic transmission; these were prone to overheating and fluid transmission fires, and the sets were all withdrawn by 1969. In the second view enthusiasts trespass over the track as a two-car DMU approaches the stub terminus. This was formed of two motor cars from 333 vehicles built at Derby between 1958 and 1961. *Martin Jenkins/Online Transport Archive (both)*

With the end of steam fast approaching, many organised tours
were operated, in some instances using diesel power for part of
the itinerary. On 4 August 1968 a Stephenson Locomotive Society
special was worked by EE Type 4 No D394 as far as Manchester
Victoria, where 'Black Fives' Nos 44874 and 45107 were waiting
to take over for the next leg of the journey around Lancashire and
Yorkshire. In the background is BR Type 2 No D5156. No D394,
which by this time had received full yellow ends, was in traffic
from 1962 to 1985. *J. G. Parkinson/Online Transport Archive*

In the mid-1960s an unidentified BR Type 2 stands on Astley Bridge Viaduct, on the Bolton–Blackburn line, with a special viaduct-inspection train. Enclosed in a cage which swung out and down, engineers were able to inspect every part of the structure, including the underside of the arches. In the background is the goods station on the short former Astley Bridge branch. *John Worley/Online Transport Archive*

A fine study of Diggle Junction in August 1966 featuring one of the eight Swindon-built 'Trans-Pennine' units, with their distinctive wrap-around cab windows. Delivered to the North Eastern Region in 1960, each six-car train had four motor cars powered by two 230hp Leyland Albion engines, giving a total output of 1,840hp — ideal for tackling the demanding cross-Pennine terrain and challenging competing coach services, although the opening of the M62 motorway led to a considerable drop in traffic. The provision of a buffet car was a welcome addition, but this facility was withdrawn in 1972. The last of the 'Trans-Pennine' units was taken out of service in 1984; sadly, none passed into preservation. *Phil Tatt/Online Transport Archive*

LEFT

In the Peak District, Derby-built BR Type 2 No D5209 is seen on a freezing day in early 1967. For many years pairs of these locomotives were tasked with hauling heavy trains of hopper wagons loaded with limestone from this area to the chemical works at Northwich. At this time some freight diagrams were still worked by steam, mostly grimy '8Fs'. Having arrived with a load of empties, No D5209 was running round prior to coupling up to a sister locomotive before departing. First assigned to Toton, it was in traffic from 1963 until 1987.

Phil Tatt/Online Transport Archive

The period covered by this book witnessed the closure of hundreds of stations, some of which remained *in situ* for some time afterwards. One such was Manningham, which closed on 31 May 1965 but was still largely intact a year later when 'Peak' No D106 passed through with a cross-country train from Bristol to Bradford Forster Square. The motive-power depot on the right would close in April 1967. Opened by the Midland Railway in 1872, this featured a brick-built roundhouse and latterly catered for steam and diesel power. No D106 was in traffic from 1961 to 1989. *Gavin Morrison*

Overlooked by derelict quarry buildings, a Cravens three-car unit leaves Millers Dale for Tideswell *en route* to Buxton on 2 March 1967. Perched high above the village, the five-platform station closed to all traffic in March 1967; then in July 1968 the whole of this picturesque line was abandoned when the remaining expresses were re-routed. Note the LMS signals on the left and the Midland Railway signal on the right. Some buildings survive today, and the trackbed forms part of the Monsal Trail, while a preservation scheme to reopen the entire line from Matlock to Buxton has reached as far north as Rowsley. *Martin Jenkins/Online Transport Archive*

Another station to close was Stanningley, and although it was replaced by a new facility at New Pudsey this was built some distance away and arguably serves a different locale. On the last day, 30 December 1967, a Metro-Cammell DMU forming the 3.2pm Bradford Exchange–Leeds Central leaves gas-lit 'Stanningley for Farsley' and passes the complex of mills (right). The main station building survives today. *J. M. Ryan*

This July 1963 scene at Leeds Holbeck features different variants of 'Peak'. To the fore is Derby-built No D27, which has split headcode boxes either side of the nose, although this was unnecessary, as most of these locomotives were built without nose-end doors. Behind is one of the later series with a centrally located four-character display. The paint scheme on the 'Peaks' was enhanced by a relief band in pale blue/green. No D27 was in traffic from 1961 to 1981.
Phil Tatt/Online Transport Archive

One of the short-lived Beyer Peacock-built 'Claytons', No D8607, is pictured at Barrow Hill shortly after delivery. Each section either side of the central cab housed a 450hp engine, most being of Paxman manufacture. Owing to poor reliability the 'Claytons' were phased out in the period 1968-71. No D8607, which ended its days in Scotland, was in service only from October 1964 to October 1971. Today Barrow Hill is a maintenance depot for main-line locomotives and shunters as well as being a preservation centre. *Phil Tatt/Online Transport Archive*

ABOVE

Sporting yellow and black 'wasp' ends, two of the ubiquitous 350hp diesel-electric 0-6-0 shunters built at various BR workshops from 1952 are seen at work within Manvers Main Colliery, near Mexborough, on 23 October 1971. Both were built at Darlington – No D4033 (leading) in 1960, No D3068 in 1953. The latter was withdrawn in 1980, but No D4033 (in its later guise as 08865) remains in stock with freight operator DB Schenker. *E. V. Richards*

ABOVE

In order to provide sufficient power to move heavy loads within the extensive Tinsley Yard in Sheffield six 350hp 0-6-0 shunters were rebuilt at Darlington during 1965 to work as permanently coupled pairs, one of each pair having its cab removed so that both were controlled from the remaining cab. Larger buffer-beams were also provided. Initially the two halves were coupled back-to-back, but they were soon reconfigured nose-to-tail, with the remaining cab at one end. This photograph taken in August 1968 shows two of the three 0-6-0+0-6-0 combinations. Nearer the camera is No D4500 (the former D3698 and D4188) and behind it is No D4502 (formerly D3697 and D4187). With the demise of coal and wagonload traffic the need for large marshalling yards disappeared, and these locomotives succumbed to the scrapman's torch during the period 1982-6. *E. V. Richards*

RIGHT

On 23 May 1965 No D7545 waits to leave Sheffield Midland with a stopping train for Manchester Central via Chinley, comprising three ex-LMS carriages. Built at Derby and looking clean and sparkling, this BR Type 2 had entered service earlier in the month and would remain in stock until June 1985. *E. V. Richards*

BELOW

In 1964 EE Type 3 No D6713 heads a Harwich boat train past Blackmoor Crossing, near Penistone, on the former main line between Manchester and Sheffield, which had been electrified in 1954 using the 1500V DC system. On the right is a Manchester, Sheffield & Lincolnshire Railway signalbox dating from 1873.

Following the dramatic decline of cross-Pennine coal traffic during the 1960s any plans to modernise the Woodhead line were abandoned, and although it was not listed for closure in the Beeching Report passenger traffic ceased in 1970, freight following in 1981. *Phil Tatt/Online Transport Archive*

LEFT

Two stations are visible in this view: in the distance is New Holland Pier, where passengers and vehicles could gain access to the Humber ferries, whilst in the foreground is New Holland Town. Connecting them was the long timber pier which had been rebuilt in the 1920s to accommodate three tracks. In April 1965 a pair of Derby-built DMU sets waits to leave for Cleethorpes. In the distance can be seen one of the trio of 'Castle' paddle-steamers built between 1934 and 1940. Vehicles using the ferry ran along the elevated platforms. Latterly this whole structure was in a parlous state, and its use by trains ceased on 24 June 1981, following the opening of the Humber Bridge. Since 1998 a large grain and animal-feed terminal has occupied part of the site. *Phil Tatt/Online Transport Archive*

BELOW

Northbound on a stopping service to Doncaster, a Derby three-car DMU calls at Retford in April 1965. The station layout here would be radically altered later in the year, the new arrangement involving platforms on two levels and a bridge replacing a flat crossing (just beyond the signalbox and signal bracket in this view). Among the connecting curves that would disappear was that being used by the Sheffield–Gainsborough DMU seen in the background, which allowed the train access to the platform on the right. *Phil Tatt/Online Transport Archive*

Gamston Bank, south of Retford, was an ideal location for photographers, offering views unimpeded by fences and lineside poles. This 1959 close-up of the *Deltic* prototype, in its eye-catching livery of powder blue with two parallel white bands along the sides and three bright white 'speed whiskers' beneath a central headlight, was taken when the locomotive was undergoing trials on the East Coast main line. *Deltic* had been built by EE as a speculative venture with a view to obtaining future orders both at home and overseas, and the pair of engines capable of providing 3,300hp were supplied by D. Napier & Sons, an EE subsidiary. Officially DP1, this locomotive was in service from November 1955 (at first mostly hauling freight trains) until March 1961, after which it was donated to the Science Museum. Nowadays it forms part of the National Railway Museum collection. *Derek Penney*

The operating area for the EE Type 4s was extended considerably as they began to take over express workings on the East Coast main line. During his 1959 visit to Gamston Bank Derek Penney recorded this view of No D206 in charge of an up train, the carriage liveries reflecting the changeover from carmine-and-cream to crimson lake. New in July 1958, the locomotive would remain in traffic until March 1983. *Derek Penney*

Seen shortly after delivery in June 1961 is No D9007 in charge of another up express. Allocated to Finsbury Park shed, it entered service bearing the name *Pinza*, after a popular racehorse which won The Derby in 1953. This view shows to good effect the 'Deltic' livery, with white cabs and light-green skirt. No D9007 survived in traffic until the end of 1981. *Derek Penney*

ABOVE

We now move across country to Toton, where EE Type 1 No D8138 is seen posing outside the depot shortly after delivery in April 1966, the photograph showing to good advantage the attractive livery, before the grey roof became discoloured. This was one of the later members of the class, with four-character headcode boxes built into the nose end. With their 1,000hp engines and single cabs these rugged workhorses were designed to work all manner of freight traffic, including pick-up goods from then-numerous station yards. As traffic patterns changed they often worked in pairs (usually nose-to-nose, to improve visibility) and were occasionally assigned to passenger duties, despite their lack of steam-heating equipment. This example would remain operational until 1998. *Alan Murray-Rust/Online Transport Archive*

ABOVE

During the years covered by this book the workforce at Derby designed and built many hundreds of diesel locomotives and DMUs, some of which were photographed during organised visits. Seen here outside the Test House is brand-new No D5020, first of the production run of BR Type 2s, ordered whilst the 20 Pilot Scheme machines were still under construction. The off-white band was applied to all members of the class except for No D5000. This example survived until August 1975.

G. W. Morant/Online Transport Archive

ABOVE

As a BR employee John McCann was able to photograph rare workings during his time at the Railway Technical Centre at Derby, and on 29 October 1960 he recorded a series of views of a test train at Chellaston & Swarkestone station, closed in 1930. In charge were a couple of standard Type 2s, behind which was a dynamometer car. Built in 1960, No D5135 (leading) was

withdrawn in early 1976. The former Midland Railway Melbourne branch was used by the military during World War 2 to give engineers the opportunity to practise running, demolishing and rebuilding railways. It duly reverted to civilian use, the last sections being finally abandoned in 1980.
J. B. C. McCann/Online Transport Archive

LEFT

Amongst John McCann's early colour images is a photograph taken at Rugby of the Fell locomotive (No 10100) on its way to an exhibition in London in 1954. This diesel-mechanical 4-8-4 was constructed at Derby Works following a concept developed by Lt Col L. F. R. Fell. It had nose ends, two driving cabs and four 500hp Paxman engines. After being released for trial runs in the summer of 1950, the wheel arrangement was altered in 1952 to a 4-4-4-4 by the removal of the centre coupling rods. This experimental machine was scrapped after catching fire in 1958.
J. B. C. McCann/Online Transport Archive

On 2 January 1965 a Metro-Cammell DMU heading for Rugeley Trent Valley, on the West Coast main line, calls at Rugeley Town. This view was recorded shortly before the passenger service between Birmingham New Street and Rugeley Trent Valley was abandoned (later the same month) and the station closed. However, the line remained open for goods, especially the bulk movement of coal to Rugeley Power Station, and this facilitated its eventual reopening for passengers in stages between 1989 and 1998. *Martin Jenkins/Online Transport Archive*

Another view on the same line features one of the 20 two-car low-density Park Royal-built DMUs at Cannock whilst working the 6.10pm from Birmingham New Street to Rugeley Trent Valley on 15 September 1964. Considered non-standard, the Park Royal sets were prone to bodywork problems resulting from engine vibration, although some gave up to 25 years' service, the last being withdrawn in 1983. This one would have been based at Walsall Rycroft shed. *John Ryan*

In the period 1950-4 the Southern Region built three prototype 1Co-Co1 diesel-electric locomotives (Nos 10201-3) intended for high-speed use on Waterloo–Bournemouth/Exeter services. After various trials the SR decided not to use diesel power on its principal expresses, so Nos 10201-3 were transferred to the London Midland Region. In this view No 10201 – by now in overall BR green with orange and black lining – was working a mixed southbound freight through Atherstone station on 24 September 1960. Non-standard and prone to increasing technical problems, all three were withdrawn during 1962/3 and later scrapped. The 16-cylinder English Electric engine design used to power these locomotives was later developed for use in the EE Type 4. *Peter Jackson*

LEFT

Drawing into Birmingham New Street on 21 August 1967 is No D13, one of the first of the production run of 127 2,500hp BR/Sulzer Type 4s. Although many of the early 'Peaks' shared the split headcode configuration, this locomotive was one of only five (Nos D11-15) to have the communicating doors which this feature was designed to accommodate. Built at Derby, it was in traffic from 1960 to 1986. Since this photograph was taken New Street has been twice rebuilt.
E. V. Richards

BELOW

Heading south from Oxford, Brush Type 4 No D1747 heads a long train of vans on a inter-regional working. Thanks to the ongoing rail-modernisation programme, scenes like this would slowly disappear as once-extensive goods yards were closed or rationalised, loose-coupled trains of vans and wagons displaced and signals, signal gantries and signalboxes rendered redundant. Brush-built No D1747 was in traffic from 1964 to 2000.
Phil Tatt/Online Transport Archive

Still around in the early days of the 'green diesel' revolution were these railcars ordered by the Great Western Railway for branch-line and cross-country work, the first 18 of which were built by Park Royal and began entering service in 1934. Between 1940 and 1942 these were joined by additional cars, also built at Swindon but with more austere bodies, of which W19W-W33W had two 105hp AEC engines and pre-selector gearboxes. One such car, W21W, is seen in crimson and cream livery at Tenbury Wells shortly after the section thence to Woofferton Junction had closed, in late July 1961; services on the surviving 14 miles to Bewdley continued on a much-reduced timetable until July 1962, the last of these streamlined vehicles being withdrawn the same year.
E. C. Bennett/Online Transport Archive

A few of the former GWR railcars were repainted into the new green livery, complete with 'speed whiskers'. This one was photographed at Cleobury Mortimer on 18 July 1960. *Neil Davenport*

In 1958 railbuses replaced steam on the branches from Kemble to Tetbury (7¼ miles) and Cirencester Town (4¼ miles). Despite opening new halts and attracting new custom both lines closed in April 1964, although freight continued on the latter for another year. Service was provided by four of the five AC Cars railbuses, which were powered by 150hp engines. These were stationed at Swindon, and one, W79976, is seen at Kemble in August 1963. After the closures they eventually ended up in Scotland, where all would be withdrawn by early 1968.
Harry Luff/Online Transport Archive

As part of the 1955 Modernisation Programme a pair of Derby 'Lightweights' with driving cabs at each end took over the Banbury (Merton Street)–Buckingham section of the 21¾-mile cross-country line to Bletchley in August 1956. Although new halts were opened, and ridership increased by 400%, the service ceased in 1961. In the first photograph, taken in 1957, M79901 prepares to depart Merton Street with the 3.45pm to Buckingham. Portable steps were needed to provide ease of access to and from the wooden platforms. Following closure of the Banbury–Buckingham section the 'Lightweights' were transferred to the surviving portion between Buckingham and Bletchley. In the second view, dating from June 1964, M79900 pauses at Padbury with the 5.22pm from Bletchley. The twin exhaust pipes, fitted at one of each car, are clearly visible. The single platform station, with its low-storey brick building, had only one siding (on the left), and from 1942 until its closure to passengers in September 1964 (freight traffic having ceased in January) a long-serving lady was the only member of staff. The track was not lifted immediately after closure, so in 1966 it was possible to stable the Royal Train on the rusting rails at Padbury.
Marcus Eavis/Online Transport Archive

Waiting to leave Bletchley in 1958 on a train to Euston is No 10001, one of two prototype Co-Co main-line diesel locomotives built by the LMS at Derby Works. The first, No 10000, emerged in November 1947 in a predominantly black livery complete with 'L M S' legend; No 10001 followed in July 1948 but without the LMS lettering. The design, overseen by LMS Chief Mechanical Engineer H. G. Ivatt, was greatly influenced by English Electric. Operating singly or in multiple, the two locomotives was subjected to a series of rigorous performance tests. In 1956 both were repainted in standard green following overhauls at Derby Works. Each of these prototypes had an EE power unit capable of producing 1,600hp, the design being similar to that used in Nos 10201-3 and the subsequent EE Type 4.
Marcus Eavis/Online Transport Archive

Listed in the Beeching report, the line from Dunstable to Hatfield finally closed in April 1965. On the last day two Cravens-built DMUs pass at a deserted Luton Bute Street station, which was relatively close to Luton Midland Road on the former MR main line, visible in the background (left); note the BRCW Type 2 on a southbound freight. Bute Street remained open for goods traffic until June 1967, but subsequently the track was lifted, and the buildings were demolished. Today most of the trackbed forms the basis of the Luton–Dunstable Busway. *Marcus Eavis/Online Transport Archive*

In the summer of 1958 Park Royal-built railbuses were introduced on two services from Bedford Midland Road – to Northampton Castle (22½ miles) and to Hitchin (16¼ miles). Unfortunately M79970-4 were not reliable and often had to be replaced before they were sent to Scotland in 1960. In the first view M79973 (also seen on page 11) passes the busy yard and signalbox near Bedford Midland Road in 1959 on the 2.26pm to Hitchin. This service was abandoned in late December 1961. The next two photographs feature the Northampton–Bedford line. The first shows a crowded railbus calling at Turvey, whilst the second was taken at Olney after DMUs had replaced the problematic railbuses. This station had a two-storey stone building on the down platform and a smaller stone waiting room on the up and was gas-lit to the end. The once-busy line closed to passengers in March 1962, although freight continued to serve Olney until January 1964.
Marcus Eavis/Online Transport Archive (1 and 3); Harry Luff/Online Transport Archive (2)

In the summer of 1961 a three-car DMU calls at Wigston South on a service from Leicester to Rugby. This station, with its staggered platforms located either side of a level crossing, had opened as early as 1840 and was formerly on the MR main line. The passenger service latterly consisted of seven weekday trains in each direction and was withdrawn altogether at the beginning of January 1962, although the local coal depot remained open until May 1966. The DMU vehicles were among 300 built by BRCW of Smethwick that could be operated in two-, three- and four-car formations, the motor cars each having two 150hp engines.
Neil Cossons/Online Transport Archive

ABOVE

During the 'green' years other liveries were tried experimentally on certain types of locomotive. Brush Type 2 No D5579 was painted from new in golden ochre (also described as bronze gold) with two white bands, although by the time it was photographed at Luffenham, Rutland, during Whitsun 1965, with a rake of LMS coaches, the colour combination had certainly lost its lustre. Along with sister locomotive No D5578, which was painted 'Chromatic blue', it was painted green for the first time in 1966, which year witnessed the introduction of the new Rail-blue scheme. No D5579 was in stock from 1960 until 1991. *Phil Tatt/Online Transport Archive*

Horncastle, in Lincolnshire, lost its passenger service to Woodhall Junction in 1954, although the branch remained open until April 1971 for the transportation of bulk cargoes such as petroleum and agricultural products. Shortly before the end, in the autumn of 1970, a mixed goods trundles over a level crossing the guard having to open and close the gates. EE 0-6-0 shunter No D4065, in traffic from 1961 until 1971, was among 146 locomotives of this type fitted with a 350hp Lister-Blackstone engine rather than the more common EE power unit, all being withdrawn as non-standard by 1972.
Martin Jenkins/Online Transport Archive

Although the proximity of the Royal residence at Sandringham to Wolferton station may have influenced Dr Beeching's decision not to list the 15¼-mile line from King's Lynn to Hunstanton it did not survive; despite costs being cut to the bone it closed in May 1969, the last Royal Train having run in 1966. By the end Hunstanton station had one remaining track, the goods yard and sidings to accommodate the seasonal excursion trains having been lifted. Here a pair of Derby-built two-car sets wait to return to King's Lynn.
Marcus Eavis/Online Transport Archive

ABOVE AND BELOW

The Wisbech & Upwell Tramway last carried passengers in 1952, which year saw diesel locomotives replace steam, but goods along the 5¾-mile line continued until May 1966. There were no signals but several good yards *en route*. No D2201 is seen first at on the Wisbech East Harbour branch and then heading along Outwell Road, both photographs being taken on 27 November 1965. In the second, the train has paused so that the crew can buy bread from a local shop! The line carried all manner of goods, including coal as well as tons of fruit during the season, and it was quite a sight to see a pair of locomotives hauling up to 60 loaded vans. The locomotives working this roadside tramway were required to have a cow-catchers at either end and encased side-rods; they also had to be fitted with a speed governor. Powered by a 204hp Gardner engine, No D2201 was one of four Drewry Car Co 0-6-0s that regularly worked the line and was in stock from 1952 to 1968. *John Ryan (both)*

Typical of many Beeching closures was the section from North Walsham (Main) to the Norfolk coastal town of Mundesley-on-Sea. Originally this station had been on a loop from North Walsham to Cromer, but the northern portion closed in April 1953; its alignment can be seen here in the background. The remaining 5¼ miles closed in early October 1964, a little over two months after a two-car Metro-Cammell lightweight set, E79057 nearer the camera, was photographed waiting to depart at 2.38pm. These vehicles were from the first order for DMUs built by the private sector in 1955/6 and, owing to their non-standard coupling arrangements, they were withdrawn by 1969 as branch-line closures reduced demand. *E. V. Richards*

Another line to close was that from Saxmundham to the small coastal village of Aldeburgh. Despite the introduction of DMUs in 1956 passenger traffic continued to decline, and the line would have closed sooner but for the construction of Sizewell nuclear power station which was accessed by a siding. Listed in the Beeching Report, it finally lost its passenger service in September 1966. Earlier that year, on 19 February, a 'pre-selector' Derby 'Lightweight' twin leaves Saxmundham and proceeds cautiously over the level crossing at the start of its 8¼-mile journey. Note the Yellow Diamond coupling code, which indicated these units' limited compatibility with other types of DMU. *Phil Tatt/Online Transport Archive*

Waiting to depart Harwich Parkeston Quay in February 1964
is No D5666, one of 134 Brush Type 2 A1A-A1A locomotives
assigned to the Great Eastern section of the ER for a wide range
of duties. All 263 members of the class were originally powered
by Mirrlees engines, but these were replaced from 1965 by
1,470hp EE units after the originals were found to be suffering
from fatigue. Originally allocated to March shed, No D5666 was
in traffic from November 1960 and was thus 50 years old when
scrapped in 2010. The light-grey roof and white bands were
notable features of this class. *Phil Tatt/Online Transport Archive*

Some closures attracted little attention, passing almost without
notice. However, photographers and locals were out in force on
15 June 1964, the last day of service of the five-mile line linking
Wivenhoe with the one-time fishing village of Brightlingsea, where
crowds are seen alighting from a Cravens two-car set. For years
the main revenue had been derived from the transportation of
fresh fish and the seasonal influx of holidaymakers and day-
trippers. Despite a frequent service the branch was targeted
by Beeching, ostensibly due to the cost of maintaining a swing
bridge. *Phil Tatt/Online Transport Archive*

By September 1958 the first 10 of the EE Type 4 locomotives ordered as part of the Modernisation Plan's Pilot Scheme had been assigned to the ER, five being based on the Great Eastern section, at Stratford, and five on the Great Northern. One of the former, No D204, is seen at Colchester with an express from Liverpool Street to Norwich. These heavy machines, with their 2,000hp engines, proved slow to accelerate and as such could not improve on timings achieved by the 'Britannia' Pacifics introduced in the early 1950s and, in later years, were employed largely on freight workings. This example would remain in traffic until 1984.
Marcus Eavis/Online Transport Archive

In April 1961, on the final day of passenger service on the line from Bury St Edmunds to Long Melford, Brush Type 2 No D5531 calls at Lavenham with a short southbound freight as, on the platform, the signalman prepares to hand over the tablet covering the next section of single track. For a relatively small country station Lavenham had a large goods yard, which remained open until April 1965. All buildings have now been demolished. *John Ryan*

Seen at Sudbury on 8 April 1961 is a two-car Derby 'Lightweight' (left) and one of five two-car DMUs built for BR by D. Wickham & Co in 1957. DMUs and diesel railbuses had ousted steam on passenger lines serving this area at the beginning of 1959. The section from Sudbury to Shelford closed to freight in October 1966 and to passengers in March 1967. Many years later, in 1991, Sudbury station was re-sited, and all the buildings seen here have been demolished. *John Ryan*

Five 56-seater railbuses powered by 150hp Büssing engines were purchased from German firm Waggon & Maschinenbau in 1958 and stationed at Cambridge for use on a number of lightly trafficked lines serving mostly rural farming communities, but the lack of any space for goods plus the inability to haul any vans or wagons proved a major drawback. This one is seen leaving Saffron Walden at the start of the 1¾-mile journey to the junction with the main line at Audley End. This shuttle service, along with through trains on the Stour Valley line, were withdrawn in September 1964, to be followed a few months later by the last freight trains. This particular railbus was one of three of its type to be fitted with an AEC engine and painted dark green. All were withdrawn by 1967, although four survive in preservation. *Tom Marsh/Online Transport Archive*

Specially designed for operation on the Southern Region (SR) were 98 BRCW Type 3 Bo-Bo locomotives built between 1959 and 1962 at Smethwick and fitted with 1,550hp Sulzer engines and four traction motors supplied by Crompton Parkinson. These were also the first main-line diesel locomotives to be fitted with electric train-heating equipment and SR EMU-style two-character train reporting blinds. In August 1966 No D6547 heads a Director's saloon through Faversham. This 'Crompton' entered traffic in March 1961 and is still in stock, in the fleet of the spot-hire West Coast Railway Co. *M. Knight/Online Transport Archive*

Designed to replace steam on some of its non-electrified lines, the SR introduced a series of diesel-electric multiple-units (DEMUs), which were radically different from the DMUs on the rest of the network in having the diesel engine above the carriage frames in the motor car. Built at Eastleigh Works, the '2H'- and '3H'-series units were first introduced on routes in Hampshire, but four '2H' two-car units entered service in 1958 on the Ashford–Hastings line and the Bexhill West and New Romney branches, and one of these, No 1122, is seen at New Romney & Littlestone-on-Sea in January 1962. During World War 2 this branch, which had been upgraded in the 1930s to serve developing holiday resorts, carried a considerable volume of military traffic. Goods finished in 1965, and the passenger service in March 1967, although a section was retained to transport nuclear waste from Dungeness Power Station. Today nothing remains of this station. *Phil Tatt/Online Transport Archive*

DEMUs were introduced on the Horsham–Brighton line in 1964. Despite having a regular-interval service this closed in March 1966, although the section to Southwater remained open for goods until 1982. Pausing at Steyning in the summer of 1965, No 1303 was from a fleet of 19 Class 3D 'East Sussex' sets built at Eastleigh and fitted with 600hp EE engines. The yellow warning panel was located between the recesses housing the hoses and jumper cables. The substantial station, with its two-storey building, overbridge and imposing water tower, was subsequently demolished. *Marcus Eavis/Online Transport Archive*

Green action at Redhill in May 1967 as the driver of 'Hampshire' DEMU No 1115 carefully reverses past a '2-BIL' EMU in preparation for a return cross-country run to Reading. The large 'V' on the front indicated the end of the unit where the luggage compartment was located; upon the application of yellow warning panels this gave way to an inverted black triangle, as seen here on the EMU. *Fred Ivey*

Crossing to East London and Bush Hill Park, a two-car Wickham DMU was undergoing test runs when photographed during the winter of 1957/8. With the tail lamp in position it was about to reverse. These vehicles were of lightweight construction, each two-car unit consisting of a Driving Motor Brake Second and Driving Trailer Composite. Only five sets were built, two being sold to the Trinidad Government Railway in 1961. The last example to operate on BR was withdrawn 10 years later. One set is preserved after serving as the ER General Manager's saloon. *Frank Hunt/LRTA (London Area)*

Organised visits to BR premises offered an opportunity to see a wide range of equipment, and this view of No D6703 was recorded at Stratford depot in East London. This locomotive was one of an initial batch of 30 EE Type 3 Co-Cos that were used to replace steam on GE express passenger services, these early examples all having nose-end gangway doors and split headcode boxes. Although initially problems were experienced with the bogies, this class enjoyed a high degree of reliability, and some remain in service today; dating from late 1960, No D6703 survives in preservation as 37003. Partially visible on the left is No D5550, a Brush Type 2 delivered in 1959. The whole of the former depot and works site at Stratford was later cleared to make way for the Olympic Park. *Phil Tatt/Online Transport Archive*

Also pictured at Stratford is No D2905, one of a small batch of 350hp NBL 0-4-0 diesel-hydraulic shunters delivered during 1958/9, mostly for work on the Eastern and London Midland Regions. After a relatively short life the entire class of 14 locomotives was withdrawn in February 1967. *Phil Tatt/Online Transport Archive*

ABOVE AND BELOW

Among the Pilot Scheme diesels ordered as part of the 1955 Modernisation Plan were a batch of 10 EE Bo-Bos built at Vulcan Foundry, each with a single 1,100hp Napier Deltic engine. When the first of these 'Baby Deltic' locomotives was delivered it was found to be overweight for the intended routes, but by the end of 1959 Nos D5900-9 were all assigned to King's Cross suburban services. However, as a result of recurring engine failures all were soon laid up at Stratford Works, where Nos D5903 and D5902 are seen in the first view. Having been refurbished at Vulcan Foundry they reappeared during 1963/4 painted in the two-tone-green livery applied to the Type 5 'Deltics' and with four-character headcode boxes, the nose-end doors having been removed. In the second view, recorded in 1964, Nos D5906 and D5903 are being prepared at Stratford before being despatched to Finsbury Park. The whole class was withdrawn in the years 1968-71 as part of the traction-rationalisation programme, most soon being scrapped; No D5901 was transferred to the Research Department at Derby but was itself later scrapped. *Harry Luff/Online Transport Archive; Phil Tatt/Online Transport Archive*

An impressive view at St Pancras, with 'Britannia' Pacific No 70052 *Firth of Tay* waiting to depart on a railtour in April 1965. On the right is a BR Type 2 on a local train. Despite the implementation of the Modernisation Plan steam locomotives continued to be built until 1960; the last 'Britannia' entered service in 1954, and most were scrapped after relatively short lives. In contrast the last of the BR-built Type 2 diesels, introduced from 1958 onwards, would survive until 1987.
Phil Tatt/Online Transport Archive

As part of the 1955 Modernisation Plan the busy commuter line between St Pancras and Bedford Midland Road was scheduled for electrification. In the interim the non-corridor steam hauled stock was replaced by a fleet of four-car high-density DMUs made up of 60 motor cars and 60 trailers, all of which emerged from Derby Works during 1959, each of the motor cars having two powerful (238hp) eight-cylinder Rolls-Royce engines coupled to hydraulic transmission.

Despite problems with the engines and the transmission these sets operated the 'Bedpan' line until electrification in 1984. Here Driving Motor Brake Second M51631 is seen at Bedford Midland Road. Note that it still has the ubiquitous Blue Square coupling code; subsequently these units would receive a Red Triangle classification because of difficulties experienced when operating diesel-mechanical and diesel-hydraulic units in multiple.
Phil Tatt/Online Transport Archive

Another short-lived class ordered as part of the Pilot Scheme were the 10 Type 1 Bo-Bo locomotives built by NBL and powered by 800hp Paxman engines. No D8400-9 spent their entire working lives from 1958 to 1968 in the London area — latterly at Stratford, so that they could be despatched to the works following all-too-frequent breakdowns, which saw them relegated to local trip work and lightly loaded cross-London freights. In June 1960 No D8408 draws into Cannon Street with an enthusiasts' special. This view clearly shows the grey applied to the front of the driver's cab. *Phil Tatt/Online Transport Archive*

The Brush Type 2s were assigned to the Eastern and North Eastern Regions, No D5649 being almost brand-new when photographed at King's Cross in the autumn of 1960. This was the most common variant, with the roof-mounted four-character headcode box; 40 of the earliest members of the class were delivered with discs, although some of these were later fitted with headcode boxes. The centre axle of each of the six-wheeled bogies was unpowered, giving the axle arrangement A1A-A1A. No D5649 was in traffic from 1960 to 1991. *Geoffrey Morant/Online Transport Archive*

In August 1959 Jack Wyse photographed several new diesel locomotives at King's Cross, our first view featuring three-month-old 'Baby Deltic' No D5902. Star of the second scene is four-month old No D6109, from the Pilot Scheme batch of 10 NBL Type 2 Bo-Bos (Nos D6100-9) allocated initially to Hornsey depot for working GN suburban services out of King's Cross; later examples were assigned to the GE Section and to Scotland, where the entire class would ultimately be concentrated in order to be near the NBL works in Glasgow.
W. J. Wyse/LRTA (London Area) (both)

Responding to the British Transport Commission's announcement that it intended placing orders for a large Type 4 diesel-electric locomotive with both steam and electric heating capability, the Brush Traction Co designed and built an experimental locomotive powered by two Maybach MD655 engines. Named after the company works in Loughborough and bearing the Brush emblem on the side, *Falcon* was given the unusual stock number D0280 (derived from its Brush works number, 280) and painted lime green and chocolate brown. Following trials in revenue-earning service, which commenced in October 1961, it was allocated to Sheffield Darnall shed in April 1962. Here it is seen arriving at King's Cross with a Pullman service from Sheffield Midland on 31 July 1962. Eventually the locomotive was sold to BR, which overhauled it and renumbered it D1200, running it until 1975, but efforts to preserve it were frustrated by a contractual requirement that the locomotive be scrapped following withdrawal. *Bruce Jenkins*

Transition time at King's Cross in June 1961, featuring two kings of speed. Delivered earlier in the month to Edinburgh's Haymarket shed, 'Deltic' No D9004 waits to head north with an Anglo-Scottish express, although the lack of a corridor connection between locomotive and train precluded its running non-stop, as crews could not be changed *en route*. Straining for the 'off' at the adjacent platform is 'A4' No 60008 *Dwight D. Eisenhower*, one of a fleet of 35 streamlined Pacifics introduced by the London & North Eastern Railway from 1935 and among six to survive in preservation. *Bruce Jenkins*

As more EE Type 4s were delivered, and initial restrictions lifted, significant numbers were allocated to the LMR to replace steam on a range of main-line express passenger duties prior to electrification. No D316 was one of those constructed at Darlington by Robert Stephenson & Hawthorns and is seen in original condition inside the old Euston station alongside 'Royal Scot' No 46165 *The Ranger (12th London Reg.)*.
Phil Tatt/Online Transport Archive

On 10 May 1961 BR/Sulzer Type 2 No D5021 approaches Willesden Junction with the 6.12pm Euston–Bletchley. The platforms on the main line closed in 1962, while the water column would soon be surplus to requirements. Built at Derby and placed in service in August 1959, No D5021 was to remain in traffic until August 1975. *C. Firminger, courtesy Bob Bridger*

Towards the end of the 'green diesel' era a powerful, high-speed, diesel-electric Co-Co prototype underwent a series of stringent tests on passenger and freight trains. Although it was built by Hawker Siddeley (which owned Brush) and powered by a 4,000hp Sulzer engine BR had considerable input into its design. HS4000 *Kestrel* had a stylish body with wrap-around cab windows and was aimed at the domestic and overseas market. Photographed at Cricklewood on a depot open day on 12 July 1969, it was eventually sold in 1971 for further service in the USSR. *Neil Davenport*

An early diagram for the Type 2 Co-Bos was the 'Condor', a new block freight introduced in March 1959 to transport mini-containers from North London to Glasgow (the name being a contraction of 'containers door-to-door'). Initially locomotives were operated in multiple, crews using the front-end communicating doors during the 10-hour journey. This rare view shows Nos D5717 and D5711 in typically smoky form as they storm away from Hendon in July 1959, just months before disappointing loadings led to the use of a single Co-Bo. Note the wrap-around cab windows, the broad duck-egg-blue band and the special 'Condor' headboard attached to No D5717. Both locomotives were withdrawn in September 1968. *Bruce Jenkins*

When introduced in 1952 the privately financed ACV Demonstration Train was painted two-tone grey with a red stripe, as seen in the first view at Harrow & Wealdstone in April 1954, car M79742 being nearest the camera. Hailed by BR as the first British lightweight train, this formation of four-wheeled vehicles was, in reality, a cross between a railbus and a DMU. The bodywork was built by Park Royal, the underframes by AEC, power being provided by the latter's well-proven bus engine. Despite the rough riding of the prototype BR ordered two further sets, which entered service in 1955; these differed from the original in having quarterlights (instead of drop-down windows) and in lacking skirting panels. Soon dubbed 'Flying Bricks', on account of the angular design of their bodywork, they were all assigned to the LMR, where from 1955 vehicles from the three sets were sometimes intermixed. In the second photograph, taken in 1957, Driving Motor M79740M (now minus side valances) from the original set leads a three-car formation at Watford Junction, whilst in the third, taken on the same day, a 'Flying Brick' dips and sways near Bricket Wood, on the short line between Watford Junction and St Albans. All were withdrawn in February 1959, although they remained relatively intact for some years thereafter.
Nigel Davenport (1); Marcus Eavis/Online Transport Archive (2 and 3)

ABOVE

Whilst recording events marking the centenary of the London Underground on 26 May 1963 Marcus Eavis took this photograph of a rake of Cravens-built 'A' stock on the Metropolitan Line being overtaken by a Derby-built DMU near Amersham, on a section of line once owned jointly with the Great Central Railway. This was one of 41 four-car units which replaced steam on Marylebone suburban services, each driving motor having two 230hp Leyland Albion engines. Many of these high-density DMUs were later refurbished and survived until the early 1990s.
Marcus Eavis/Online Transport Archive

ABOVE

In an attempt to obtain orders for new generation of Type 4 locomotives a striking private prototype was financed jointly by BRCW, AEI and Sulzer. Powered by a 2,750hp engine, it was named *Lion* and painted overall white (hardly ideal for a locomotive) with gold lining and numbers. This photograph was taken on 28 May 1962 whilst the locomotive, numbered D0260, was at Marylebone for inspection by the BR Board as part of the formal handover from the builders. Unfortunately no orders were forthcoming, and after hauling relatively few passenger trains *Lion* was returned to its owners in early 1964 and dismantled. The failure of this project hastened the demise of BRCW. *Tom Marsh/Online Transport Archive*

Having just crossed Chelsea Bridge, No D8221 heads a mixed freight past a GWR lower-quadrant signal on 15 July 1961. The locomotive was one of 44 BTH Type 1 diesel-electric Bo-Bo locomotives designed for branch-line and local freight operation. Ordered from the Clayton Equipment Co, Nos D8200-43 were delivered in two batches between 1957 and 1961. Power was provided by an 800hp Paxman engine driving BTH electrical equipment. The class was withdrawn between March 1968 and March 1971 as freight traffic declined, No D8221 being among the last to go.
Jim Oatway

On 15 August 1973 EE Type 3 No 6965, having lost its 'D' prefix following the end of steam, pauses beneath the impressive signal gantry at Kensington Olympia as it waits to depart with an inter-regional train of oil tankers. The locomotive still retained green livery at this time, albeit with the addition of full yellow ends. One of the later examples, with roof-mounted horns and centre headcode displays, it was in traffic from 1965 to 2000.
John Laker

ABOVE

Coinciding with the end of steam on the SR, the much-photographed 'Bournemouth Belle' was scheduled for withdrawal in July 1967. Hoping for steam on the penultimate Sunday, 2 July, waiting enthusiasts were disappointed when 'The Belle' appeared just west of Clapham Junction with its rake of brown and cream Pullman coaches hauled by Brush Type 4 No D1926. Having entered traffic in January 1966, this locomotive would be withdrawn in 1996 and scrapped two years later. *Marcus Eavis/Online Transport Archive*

ABOVE

To provide the necessary power for hauling heavy trains the BRCW Type 3 'Cromptons' were often coupled as pairs. On 4 August 1966 Nos D6537 and D6532, both new in 1960 and destined to remain in traffic until 1993, thunder through Micheldever with a ake of empty oil tankers bound for Fawley. The photograph was taken when the track layout through Micheldever was being 'rationalised' as part of the Waterloo–Southampton–Bournemouth electrification, the work also entailing demolition of the platform signalbox. During World War 2 Micheldever was home to a major rail-served Royal Ordnance depot which provided supplies for the D-Day landings. *E. V. Richards*

Colour photographs of prewar shunters are relatively rare. Designed as part of an attempt to begin replacing its scores of steam shunters, this was one of a batch of three diesel-electric 0-6-0s built by the Southern Railway at Ashford in 1937 and equipped with 350hp EE engines. Originally numbered 1-3, they became 15201-3 following nationalisation. This view of No 15201 was recorded at Eastleigh Works shortly before the locomotive was withdrawn from capital stock in November 1964, following which it survived in departmental use for a brief period. *Phil Tatt/Online Transport Archive*

No D2995 was one of 14 diesel-electric shunters designed to replace the steam locomotives working in and around Southampton Docks. Placed in traffic from Eastleigh depot in 1962, Nos D2985-98 were built by Ruston & Hornsby and powered by 275hp Paxman engines. In 1967 No D2995 was moving empty stock along Platform Road, Southampton, under the watchful eye of the pilotman, standing on the front step. The docks target number (8) visible on one of the front lamp-irons was also displayed at the rear. As the port's rail system declined most of these 0-6-0s were eventually sold to private industry. D2995 is one of six of this class now in preservation. *Marcus Eavis/Online Transport Archive*

The first diesel to take up residence on the Isle of Wight was No D2554, one of a class of 69 0-6-0 shunters built by Hunslet in the years 1955-61 and powered by 204hp Gardner engines. Allocated to Ryde depot at the time of electrification in 1966, it was used for departmental and engineering work and is seen at Sandown on a permanent-way train in June 1970. In traffic from 1956, it outlasted all other members of its class by many years and passed into preservation following eventual withdrawal in 1985. *E. V. Richards*

In March 1966 '3H' DEMU No 1132 approaches Woolston on a Southampton–Portsmouth stopping service. This was one of seven three-car units built at Eastleigh in 1962, each driving motor having a 600hp EE engine. Known as 'Berkshire' units, they had started life on the Reading–Salisbury service and had larger guard's vans than earlier examples of the same design. In the background is the Grade II Listed station built in the Italianate style for the London & South Western Railway in 1866. During World War 2 the station area was bombed when the nearby Spitfire factory was attacked. The large goods yard, still handling domestic coal supplies when this photograph was taken, was closed in 1967. *Phil Tatt/Online Transport Archive*

From 1964 until replaced (in 1971) by BRCW Type 3s Swindon-built 'Warships' worked inter-regional services from Exeter to Waterloo via Salisbury. For a time in the mid-1960s the WR used a maroon livery for its express diesels, many 'Warships' receiving this livery on repaint, and most 'Westerns' sporting it from new. This 'Warship' is very much off its normal route, having been assigned to work a Royal Train to Bournemouth, the stock of which can be seen in the down platform as the locomotive runs round. Note the Royal headcode 1X00. *Bruce Jenkins*

One of the less-mundane duties for the various classes of 204hp 0-6-0 shunter was to move lengthy boat trains along the twisting Weymouth Quay Tramway. The first view focuses on No D2295 caught amidst all the dockside activity as goods are off-loaded from a vessel recently arrived from the Channel Islands. This diesel-mechanical 0-6-0 was one of a class of 142 shunters supplied by the Drewry Car Co, construction of which was sub-contracted, in this case to Robert Stephenson & Hawthorns. The hand-operated warning bell, which was rung continuously whilst the locomotive was on the move, can be seen behind the exhaust stack. In the second scene BR Doncaster-built No D2397 edges cautiously along Custom House Quay on a summer's day in 1965 with the 4pm Weymouth–Waterloo boat train. One of the two railwaymen walking in front carries a furled red flag, which he will use to control movements at road crossings. Note the colourful array of British-built vehicles on the left. Dating from 1960, No D2295 was withdrawn in 1971 and sold for further service in Italy, whilst No D2397 was in traffic from 1961 to 1987. *J. L. Stevenson; Marcus Eavis/ Online Transport Archive*

Gloucester RCW built several batches of DMU for BR, including 28 three-car units featuring motor cars at either end, each of which was powered by two 150hp engines. The units had been specially designed to compete with long-distance coaches as well as to provide comfort comparable with the steam-hauled stock they were replacing on cross-country routes, some of which were of considerable distance. Included were toilets, a buffet and a large guard's compartment, and examples of these units were in service from 1958 to 1995. For a period during the steam-to-diesel transition these 'Gloucesters', worked as coupled sets of six cars. They appeared on WR suburban services in and out of Paddington, sometimes with the addition of an adapted former GWR corridor coach to increase capacity. Seen at a somewhat deserted Paddington in April 1963 is a six-car formation, Driving Motor Second W51101 being nearest the camera. *Phil Tatt/Online Transport Archive*

As most London termini were located close to large locomotive sheds and carriage sidings, locomotive movements and empty-stock workings were interspersed with scheduled trains. In this photograph taken from Royal Oak station an unidentified 'Castle' 4-6-0 is coupled to aptly named 'Warship', No D842 *Royal Oak*. The latter was one of 33 'Warships' (Nos D833-65) with two 1,100hp MAN engines and Voith transmission built under licence by NBL. Found to be less reliable than their Swindon-built counterparts, these locomotives tended to work only within the WR, and all would be withdrawn by the end of 1971. *Fred Ivey*

ABOVE AND RIGHT

In another attempt to win traffic, five luxury 'Blue Pullman' trains entered service in 1960. These comprised two six-car sets, with seats for 132 First-class passengers only, and three eight-car sets, each including two Second-class carriages. Designed by BR in conjunction with Metropolitan-Cammell, these streamlined units were intended to emulate modern European rail as well as international airline standards. The 'Pullman' experience featured personal service, advanced ticketing and reservations, kitchens, parlour cars, air-conditioning, comfortable seats (as shown in the second image), insulation and carpeting. Painted in Nanking blue with white window surrounds and displaying a new gold and red Pullman company crest on the nose, the units were assigned to three new services — the 'Midland Pullman', 'Bristol Pullman' and 'Birmingham Pullman'. In this 1965 view the last-named prepares to leave Paddington's Platform 7 with the 4.50pm to Wolverhampton Low Level, a journey scheduled to take 2 hours and 25 minutes. Unfortunately the Swiss-designed bogies gave a poor ride, especially at speed, and the LMR transferred its Pullmans to the WR in 1966. After various modifications and route alterations all were withdrawn in 1973.
Marcus Eavis/Online Transport Archive; Bruce Jenkins

As already noted, during the so-called 'green diesel' years, other colour schemes were tried, some being 'one-offs'. No D1000 *Western Enterprise*, the first of the 74 BR Type 4 'Western' C-C locomotives to enter service, on 20 December 1961, was delivered in a livery described as desert sand, which it retained when photographed at Old Oak Common in February 1964, although the yellow warning panels were a later addition. It also carried an embossed chrome version of the BR lion-and-wheel emblem below the cab window. Later repainted maroon, No D1000 would end its career in corporate Rail blue, being taken out of traffic in February 1974. Construction of the 'Westerns' was shared by the BR works at Swindon and Crewe, the former turning out Nos D1000-34 in the years 1961-4, the latter Nos D1035-73 in the period 1962-4. *Phil Tatt/Online Transport Archive*

Also pictured at Old Oak Common in February 1964 is No D6326, one of 58 NBL Type 2 B-B locomotives (D6300-57) with MAN engines, delivery of which began in January 1959 and was completed in November 1962. Although the class was largely confined to freight and secondary passenger workings all but the first six occasionally worked in multiple on main-line duties. After the decision to dispose of all diesel-hydraulic locomotives, withdrawal commenced at the end of 1967, No D6326 being stood down in October 1971 after little more than 11 years of service. *Phil Tatt/Online Transport Archive*

A common sight within the WR around London were six Driving Motor Luggage Vans built as part of a batch of 10 by Gloucester RCW in 1960 (the other four, which differed in detail, going to the LMR). Powered by two Leyland Albion 230hp engines, they were capable of hauling a number of vacuum-braked vans if required. This view of one of the vehicles, bound for Paddington on a regular parcels working from Slough, shows the gangway connection, the three large pairs of access doors and the legend 'Parcels Service' on the side. Five of the luggage vans assigned originally to the WR lasted until 1990.
Bruce Jenkins

Working the short Greenford shuttle, a two-car DMU formation calls at Ealing Broadway in 1958. To the fore is Driving Trailer Second W56297, one of nine built earlier in the year by Gloucester RCW; these could be attached to other stock with the Blue Square coupling code, notably the 20 single Gloucester railcars (W55000-19), also new in 1958, one of which can be seen bringing up the rear. The last of the driving trailers was withdrawn in 1982. The device between the rails in the foreground is the GWR Automatic Train Control system.
Marcus Eavis/Online Transport Archive

In 1960 Pressed Steel – a subsidiary of the British Motor Corporation based in Linwood, Scotland – built 16 Second-class 65-seater railcars (W55020-35) with a driving cab at each end, power being provided by two 150hp engines. Working singly on the Staines West branch and showing the exhaust pipes that were fitted at one end only, W55028 prepares to leave Colnbrook in April 1965. Two of these cars were still in service with Chiltern Railways in 2016, being the longest-serving of the many hundreds of DMU vehicles produced in the 'green' era. *Marcus Eavis/Online Transport Archive*

During World War 2 the GWR built a number of railcars at Swindon, among them 'Express Parcels' car W34W, which entered service in 1941. Powered by two 105hp AEC engines, it had a pre-selector gearbox and could carry just over 11 tons. Based at Southall, it was photographed at Slough on 14 September 1959, a year before it was withdrawn for scrap. *Ian Dunnett/Online Transport Archive*

The WR's first Type 4 diesel-hydraulic, placed in service early in 1958, was No D600 *Active*, one of five 2,000hp A1A-A1A machines (Nos D600-4) built by NBL with two high-speed MAN engines for express workings on passenger services between Paddington and the West Country, although when photographed at Reading General in 1959 it was in charge of a goods train. Also know as 'Warships', these five locomotives were very different from the lighter B-B machines (Nos D800-70), which were essentially scaled-down versions of the Deutsche Bundesbahn 'V200' design, and all five were withdrawn in December 1967. *Marcus Eavis/Online Transport Archive*

Transition time at Didcot. Seen alongside 'Modified Hall' No 6983 *Otterington Hall* is 'Hymek' Type 3 diesel-hydraulic No D7021, delivered from Beyer Peacock in February 1962. During the course of their careers the 101 locomotives of this class, introduced in the years 1961-4 and each powered by a single 1,700hp Maybach engine, undertook a range of work across the WR, albeit with few duties in Cornwall. Despite their excellent reliability record the fate of the B-B 'Hymeks' was sealed when in 1967 BR took the decision to dispense with all diesel-hydraulic classes. No D7021 was withdrawn in January 1972, the last examples surviving until early 1975. *Phil Tatt/Online Transport Archive*

LEFT

Starting in the mid-1930s, the GWR was the first of the 'Big Four' to try to increase ridership and reduce costs by introducing diesel railcars on selected routes. In 1953 the driver of Reading-based W16W carries out an inspection prior to leaving Newbury for the 12-mile run to Lambourn; powered by two 121hp AEC engines, it was one of 12 'Flying Bananas' (W5W-W16W) with Gloucester RCW bodies and was in service from 1936 to 1957. Opened as late as 1898, the Lambourn branch closed to passengers in January 1960, although freight would continue as far as Welford Park for another 13 years.
W. J. Wyse/LRTA (London Area)

BELOW

The guard watches closely as 'Hymek' No D7085 reverses an engineers' train past the 'C' Shop sidings at Swindon in June 1964. Note the oil lamp (to the left of the headcode box) and the classic GWR 'Toad' brake van. Assigned for most of its working life to South Wales, No D7085 was in service from June 1963 to October 1972. These Type 3s were the product of Beyer Peacock (Hymek) Ltd, a consortium consisting of Beyer Peacock, Bristol Siddeley Engines and J. Stone which, together with Mekydro in Germany, assembled the hydraulic transmissions – hence **Hy**draulic **Mek**ydro. *Phil Tatt/Online Transport Archive*

ABOVE

As late as April 1963 the 'A' Shop at Swindon was still repairing steam locomotives whilst also undertaking work on the WR's growing fleet of diesel-hydraulics. On the left is No 7809 *Childrey Manor,* one of a dwindling number of 'Manor' 4-6-0s still needed for work on secondary lines; centre-stage is newly delivered 'Hymek' No D7074, destined to remain in service until December 1972, while on the right is an unidentified B-B 'Warship'. *Phil Tatt/ Online Transport Archive*

BELOW

Seen under construction at Swindon in June 1964 are two of the short-lived class of 56 Type 1 diesel-hydraulics (Nos D9500-55) designed to replace steam on WR shunting and short-trip work. Fitted with 650hp Paxman Ventura 6YJX engines, these 0-6-0 locomotives were built at Swindon and entered service during 1964/5. However, their lives with BR were brief, as the duties for which they had been designed were disappearing. In the absence of any suitable work the last examples were withdrawn in April 1969, after which most were sold for further service at collieries and steel works. No fewer than 19 survive in preservation, among them No D9555, to which belongs the distinction of being the last locomotive built at Swindon.
Phil Tatt/Online Transport Archive

ABOVE

In many respects the Type 4 C-C 'Westerns' epitomised the lighter-weight diesel-hydraulics favoured by the Western Region. Designed at Swindon using experience gained with the German-influenced B-B 'Warships', the class of 74 locomotives entered service between 1961 and 1964, each powered by two 1,350hp Maybach MD655 engines driving through Voith transmission. Resplendent in its green livery, No D1004 *Western Crusader* poses at Swindon for the Kodak Works Photographic Society when almost brand-new, on 3 June 1962. It would be withdrawn just over 11 years later. Most of the 'Westerns' were painted maroon from new. *Neil Davenport*

BELOW

Seen at Swindon in the early 1960s following an overhaul and repaint is No 15104, one of six diesel-electric 0-6-0 shunters designed by the GWR but built – at Swindon – by the newly nationalised railway in 1948, each having a 350hp EE engine. Originally they also had classic GWR-style numberplates. All were withdrawn in 1967, most retaining black livery to the end. *John Piggot*

LEFT

Looking a little the worse for wear in 1967, No D1048 *Western Lady* draws to a halt at Bath Spa station, where the platform looks to be well stacked with parcels and other merchandise. From their introduction the 'Westerns' provided the power for a variety of WR express services to and from Paddington, and even after the decision to dispense with diesel-hydraulic locomotives most remained operational until the mid-1970s. First to be withdrawn were those that had not been fitted with air (in addition to vacuum) braking equipment in the mid-1960s; in contrast *Western Lady* was among the last, remaining in traffic until February 1977, and survives today in preservation. *Alan Murray-Rust/ Online Transport Archive*

BELOW

A three-car Derby suburban set passes through Hallen Marsh Junction, near Severn Beach, the ICI works being visible on the horizon. The DMU vehicles, Driving Motor Brake Second leading, were among 216 motor cars (each with two 150hp engines) and 104 trailers which began entering service in 1957. Passenger comforts on these high-density units, with their cramped seating, slam doors and drop-down windows, were limited, there being no toilets or connecting gangways. Some were later converted for parcels traffic, but others, having been refurbished, lasted until the mid-1990s. *Phil Tatt/Online Transport Archive*

The 56 diesel-hydraulic Type 1s found little work following the ruthless closure of so many branch and secondary lines. Their viability was also affected by a growth in block working, which reduced demand for long-established trip diagrams, with the result that the likes of No D9502 would remain in BR traffic for only a very short time — in this case from July 1964 to April 1969. Here the locomotive passes Lower Soudley Crossing, on the Cinderford branch, with a mixed goods on 27 April 1967. This steeply graded line, which had lost its passenger service in 1958, closed completely a few months after the photograph was taken, on 1 August 1967. *W. Potter, courtesy Martin Jenkins/Online Transport Archive*

ABOVE

Crossing into South Wales to Newport Park Junction, we find No D6867 heading north on 2 February 1966 with a string of empty unfitted 16-ton mineral wagons. These formed part of a huge fleet built by BR to eliminate the wooden-bodied wagons they had inherited from the 'Big Four' and private colliery owners after nationalisation. The EE Type 3 locomotive, built by Robert Stephenson & Hawthorns, was one of the later examples with centrally mounted headcode boxes; new in 1963, it was withdrawn in 2001.
G. D. Smith/Online Transport Archive

LEFT

No D1045 *Western Viscount* growls through Newport station on the down through line. These stylish machines were highly popular with enthusiasts, so when the last examples were about to be withdrawn in 1977 various farewell tours were organised, and seven were subsequently preserved. Most clocked up more than a million miles in traffic.
R. W. A. Jones/Online Transport Archive

Photographed before the application of 'speed whiskers', a high-density Derby-built DMU loads at Abercynon while working a Merthyr Tydfil–Barry Island service in early September 1958. Unlike the earliest examples, delivered in 1957, this three-car unit lacks a roof-mounted marker light, while in place of a central headlight there appears a two-digit headcode display. Beyond the train stood Abercynon locomotive shed, which, along with the station buildings, was later demolished.

Marcus Eavis/Online Transport Archive

An atmospheric view of Radyr Junction, recorded on 18 August 1966. With the sidings occupied by a variety of wagons and vans, a freight from Cardiff Docks is passed by a DMU heading north. No D6916 was among 180 EE Type 3s sent new to the WR from March 1963, principally for freight operation in South Wales. Placed in traffic from Swansea's Landore depot in January 1964, it was withdrawn in 2004 as No 37216 and is now preserved.

G. D. Smith/Online Transport Archive

Placed in traffic in May 1957 and destined to remain active until 1988, Derby-built No D3365 was one of the 1,193 350hp 0-6-0 shunters constructed in various BR workshops over a 10-year period from 1952. New to Cardiff Cathays depot, it was photographed working in the extensive yard east of Cardiff General in the spring of 1964, at which time steam was still very much in evidence and the sidings were occupied by a wide variety of vans and wagons. Today this location has changed completely, although the bridge in the background has only recently been replaced by Network Rail.
R. W. A. Jones/Online Transport Archive

This scene at Barry Pier was recorded on the occasion of the Warwickshire Railway Society's 'South Wales Railtour No 2', on 13 April 1968. Standing at the sole remaining platform is a Swindon-built three-car 'Cross-Country' unit, W50680 leading, its white roof dome showing clear evidence of accumulated dirt. The first of these sets, which included two Driving Motor Brake Seconds, each powered by two six-cylinder 150hp engines, entered service in March 1958, and many enjoyed a long association with South Wales. The somewhat basic Barry Pier station, which at one time provided a connection with steamers at the nearby landing stage, was reached by a tunnel from Barry Island station and closed officially in July 1976. The vessel in the background belonged to Geest Industries and would have been bringing bananas and other produce from the West Indies. *G. D. Smith/Online Transport Archive*

LEFT

Following disastrous flooding in the latter part of 1964 the meandering former GWR line from Carmarthen to Aberystwyth, already slated for closure, was truncated at Strata Florida, and steam was replaced by diesel for the final few weeks. On the last day of passenger service, in February 1965, 'Hymek' No D7030 pauses with its southbound train at the single platform at Pont Llanio so that parcels and general merchandise can be loaded. Milk traffic to the creamery at Pont Llanio continued until 1970 and to other points on the southern section of the line until 1973. No D7030 was operational from April 1962 until May 1973.
Martin Jenkins/Online Transport Archive

BELOW

One of the most delightful WR branches was the meandering 7½-mile line from Tiverton Junction to Hemyock, which, despite losing its passenger service in September 1963, remained open for general goods until 31 October 1975, revenue being derived mostly from the large creamery at Hemyock. With the erstwhile station in the foreground, an unidentified NBL Type 2 shunts at Hemyock in August 1969.

The locomotive, which had arrived with two wagons of scrap metal, would depart with a train of milk tanks, rail access to the creamery being on the north side of the station. Construction of the line had been financed by local landowners and farmers, and it continued to transport agricultural produce to the end.
Martin Jenkins/Online Transport Archive

An excellent panoramic view of Yeovil Town station, which at one time had been served by the London & South Western Railway and the GWR, services from here operating to Yeovil Junction and to Yeovil Pen Mill. From December 1964 until closure in October 1966 railbuses W79975/6, built by AC Cars in 1958, were assigned to the 1¾-mile Yeovil Town–Yeovil Junction service, and in this view, recorded shortly before the end, W79976 is leaving Town station for Junction. Following the closure of this line the railbuses ran through to Pen Mill until replaced by a single DMU vehicle, whereupon they migrated north to Scotland. As late as September 1966 Town station remained open for parcels traffic, although the locomotive shed (right) had closed in June 1965.
Marcus Eavis/Online Transport Archive

In this classic scene near Newton Abbot a westbound 'Warship' crosses the embankment opposite Shaldon as it skirts the River Teign. This was a favourite location for railway photographers, as many additional trains were operated along this busy coastal section, especially on Saturdays, to cater for the holiday trade to the numerous West Country resorts. *John Ashburner/Online Transport Archive*

ABOVE

One of the most interesting Cornish branches to survive is the steeply graded 8¾-mile single-track line from Liskeard to Looe, which involves a reversal at Coombe Junction. Listed for closure in the Beeching Report, it was ultimately reprieved. In 1965 a three-car high-density DMU waits to depart Looe on its 30-minute journey to the junction at Liskeard.

In steam days there had been no run-round facilities at the station, so locomotives had to move forward to run around within an area of sidings to the east. This view shows the original riverside station, with its single platform; in 1968 a new station was built a short distance to the north.

R. W. A. Jones/Online Transport Archive

LEFT

In the wake of the Beeching Report Cornwall lost many of its branch lines, which led to a reduction in the number of passengers using main-line services. A case in point was the attractive 5½-mile line from Lostwithiel to Fowey, on which passenger services ceased in January 1965, although the station at Fowey, here playing host to another of the single railcars built by Pressed Steel in 1960, continued to be served by goods trains from Par until 1968. Although some buildings survive the station site is now occupied by a car park, but part of the branch from Lostwithiel still handles china-clay traffic as far as a jetty at Carne Point.

Alan Murray-Rust/Online Transport Archive

A fine study of one of the 58 NBL Type 2
diesel-hydraulics allocated to the WR for
freight and secondary passenger duties.
Recently delivered No D6314 prepares to
leave Lostwithiel in the summer of 1960,
NBL's distinctive diamond-shaped builder's
plate being visible beneath the locomotive
number. On the right of the picture, adjacent
to some china-clay wagons, is '14xx'
0-4-2T No 1419, working the branch
train to Fowey. No D6314 was in traffic
from January 1960 to April 1969.
Harry Luff/Online Transport Archive

RIGHT

Among the few branches to escape the
Beeching axe was that linking the resort
of St Ives with the main line at St Erth,
where an unidentified 'Warship' is seen
awaiting departure in April 1965. Since
their introduction in 1958 'Warships'
handled a variety of West of England
expresses until the decision was taken
to dispense with all diesel-hydraulic
locomotives. As a result the last of these
Type 4s was taken out of service in 1972.
Phil Tatt/Online Transport Archive

ABOVE

In 1965 a three-car Swindon 'Cross-Country' set waits to leave the coastal resort of St Ives on its 12-minute journey to St Erth. Converted to standard gauge in 1892, this 4¼-mile branch had been the last broad-gauge passenger line to open. Listed for closure in the Beeching Report, it was eventually reprieved, although operating costs were severely curtailed, staffing levels reduced, through summer carriages discontinued, and sidings removed (by 1966); goods traffic ceased in 1963. Finally, in 1971, a basic station structure replaced the one seen here, with its distinctive curved platform. On the plus side, the line is now thriving, especially during the summer, when four-car trains operate every 30 minutes. *R. W. A. Jones/Online Transport Archive*

LEFT

This nostalgic journey through the 'green' years ends at Penzance, where No D809 is seen at the head of a five-coach train. This was one of 13 B-B 'Warships' delivered with brackets for a three-character headcode display, these fittings being later replaced by four-character indicator blinds as seen here. Named after the Admiralty warship *Champion*, it was in traffic from August 1959 to October 1971. *R. W. A. Jones/Online Transport Archive*